"Kara Powell isn't just a terrific thinker and writer about youth ministry—she knows what it's like in the trenches. This is deep impact material."

—John Ortberg, pastor and author, Menlo Park Presbyterian Church

"Kara and the team at Fuller Youth Institute have filled an important training gap with this excellent resource that moves volunteers from being chaperones to becoming shepherds. This thoroughly researched, user-friendly approach (team journals, group meeting guides, etc.) is precisely the kind of mentor-focused training that our leaders need and the kind of motivating/equipping resource that wise (and busy) youth workers want to provide but seldom have time to prepare."

—Dr. Duffy Robbins, professor of youth ministry, Eastern University

"The quality of resources coming from FYI is unparalleled these days, and *Essential Leadership* is as good as anything I've seen. Deploying an increasing number of well-cared-for adult ministry leaders is the not-so-secret key to our ability to share Jesus with kids in life-on-life relationships. Our staff who use *Essential Leadership* find it an extremely valuable asset in this multiplication strategy—a long-needed tool that will help busy people invest in their mission-partner volunteers."

—Dr. Dave Rahn, chief ministry officer, Youth for Christ/USA

"Kara Powell and the Fuller Youth Institute team continue to serve the church and our youth ministries through getting us to ask the important questions while framing answers that yield something more than scattershot busyness. *Essential Leadership* is an essential tool for building your youth ministry team into a group that forges ahead with unity, passion, knowledge, and depth in ways that will take kids deep in their faith. . . both now and for the rest of their lives."

—Dr. Walt Mueller, Center for Parent/Youth Understanding

Kara Powell
AND THE FULLER YOUTH INSTITUTE

ESSENTIAL
LEADERSHIP

"Kara Powell isn't just a terrific thinker and writer about youth ministry – she knows what it's like in the trenches. This is deep impact material."

John Ortberg
pastor and author
Menlo Park Presbyterian
Church

MINISTRY
TEAM
MEETINGS
THAT
WORK

**LEADER'S
GUIDE**

ZONDERVAN®

ZONDERVAN.com/
AUTHORTRACKER
follow your favorite authors

youth
specialties

YOUTH SPECIALTIES

Essential Leadership Leader's Guide: Ministry Team Meetings That Work
Copyright 2009 by Kara Powell

Youth Specialties resources, 1890 Cordell Ct. Ste. 105, El Cajon, CA 92020 are published by Zondervan, 5300 Patterson Ave. SE, Grand Rapids, MI 49530.

ISBN 978-0-310-66933-3

Cover design by SharpSeven Design
Interior design by Mark Novelli, IMAGO

Printed in the United States of America

09 10 11 12 13 14 15 • 20 19 18 17 16 15 14 13 12 11 10 9 8 7 6 5 4 3 2 1

This book is dedicated to the leaders who were essential to my spiritual journey as a teenager. Mike and Kristi, you are at the top of that list.

I also dedicate this book to the youth leaders who will someday be essential to my own family as Nathan, Krista, and Jessica navigate their own spiritual journeys.

This book would not have been possible without the essential contributions of Irene Cho, Chap Clark, Cynthia Eriksson, Brad Griffin, Pam King, Mark Maines, Meredith Miller, Jude Tiersma Watson, and Kimberly Williams.

CONTENTS

WELCOME TO THE ESSENTIAL LEADERSHIP LEADER'S GUIDE

I have a confession to make: I've led a lot of bad training meetings for volunteers in more than 20 years of youth ministry. I realize this might not be the best opening sentence in a book about essential leadership.

Some meetings felt like a string of announcements about upcoming events. At other times we got bogged down in a logistical quagmire (like that unforgettable 25-minute debate over whether we should schedule the senior banquet the week before or the week after Mother's Day). Still others degenerated into gossip sessions about our students' struggles (all in the name of "sharing prayer requests").

But we've had some good team meetings, too. Like the night we discussed our students' deepest longings and how both God and our ministry could meet them at their points of ultimate need. Or the time we talked about—and cried over—how to respond to students paralyzed by grief when one of our students was murdered. Or the meeting in which we revamped our upcoming trip to Mexico because we wanted to build real relationships with the locals instead of doing drive-by house building.

What's the difference between leadership team meetings that work and those that just limp along? A few simple things—

1. Essential dialogue about the real issues your kids are facing

2. Opportunities to translate your deeper insights into actual ministry practices

3. Honest conversations about how God is (or seemingly isn't) working in your own lives

While these three ingredients seem pretty simple, you're likely working too hard to stop and integrate them into every training meeting. We recognize that. We also recognize that when your team is better trained, it's highly likely you'll be able to work a little less frantically. As a result we've designed *Essential Leadership* with one simple goal: *To provide ministry team study guides that give you and your adult leadership team the essential skills you need for deeper ministry.*

Essential Thoughts and Essential Team Talk

Each chapter begins with **Essential Thoughts**, a short research-packed article that will give you and your team important background information.

Following that article, **Essential Team Talk** is a carefully crafted interactive learning experience designed to help you discuss a portion of the content of Essential Thoughts with your team—plus a whole lot more. Even if your team doesn't read the Essential Thoughts section ahead of time, they'll still get lots of essential ideas from Essential Team Talk.

Your Leader's Guide includes bold text for you to read aloud, if you choose, to guide your group discussions. You'll also see boldfaced questions for you to ask the group, and those preceded by *Q:* are printed in the Participant's Guide with room for your youth leaders to record their answers.

In a model similar to two of my previous books, *Deep Ministry in a Shallow World*[1] and *Deep Justice in a Broken World*[2], each of the nine Essential Team Talks leads your team through three steps: Now, New, and How.

Now helps you and your team consider the realities of your students and your ministry by posing the question: *What's going on now?*

New provides research-based and theologically grounded perspectives to bring new insight to those realities by asking: *What should be going on now?*

How invites your leadership team to start applying your new insights by raising the question: *How can we live this out?*

Making Them Fit Your Needs

Here's a sneak peek at the nine chapters:

- Essential Assessment: A Map That Gets Our Ministry from Here to There
- Essential Mentors: Empowering Relationships That Work
- Essential Healing: Helping Kids, Families, and Communities Toward Good Grief
- Essential Justice: Moving Beyond the News Crawl

- Essential Family Ministry: Partnering With Parents
- Essential Intergenerational Ministry: From "Big Church" to "Our Church"
- Essential Rest: Two Practices Every Leader Can Try
- Essential Holistic Ministry: Whole Ministry for the Whole Kid
- Essential Impact: Faith Beyond High School

The order of the nine guides has some logic, but you might want to strategically rearrange some to hit key calendar dates. For instance, January is an appropriate time to assess your ministry given the start of a new year—as is September at the beginning of a new school year. February is a wise month to dive into more essential justice if you have upcoming spring and summer short-term missions experiences. And family ministry might be in the air during May with Mother's Day followed shortly by Father's Day in June.

But in the midst of this logic, the reality is that while we know youth ministries, we don't know *your* youth ministry. So please adjust and reorder the chapters at will based on the particulars of your youth ministry adventure.

Getting the Most Out of These Meeting Guides

Consider the following suggestions:

1. Get our *Essential Leadership Participant's Guide* for every member of your adult team (order them at www.youthspecialties.com). Is this a shameless plug for another resource we've developed? Well, yes, but it's more than that. As we've studied youth ministries across the country, we've become convinced that the adult leaders who serve alongside you deserve to be treated as...well...adults. While you could do nine months of training using only this book, we suggest you show your high esteem for your adult leaders by making sure each of them gets a journal. The journals are complete with most of the tools provided in this resource, plus some extra ones, like blank tables and charts and journaling space for your teammates.

2. Consider the **Have More Time?** options sprinkled throughout the chapters. We've geared each study topic to take 60 to 90 minutes, but for those who want to spend more time or advance the conversation even further, use the Have More Time? suggestions to take your team deeper.

3. Go deeper either on your own or with your team using more *Essential Leadership* resources, including downloadable videos to use as part of these training sessions, available on our Web site (www.fulleryouthinstitute.org). At the Fuller Youth Institute, our mission is to leverage research into resources that elevate leaders, kids, and families. The nine meeting guides you now hold in your hands represent some of our most exciting

research, but in many ways they're only the initial steps in your journey toward essential leadership. To access free articles, curriculum, and downloadable audio resources for yourself, your team, or your students' parents, check out www.fulleryouthinstitute.org.

4. Remember—it's a process. In today's cultural adoration of fast-and-easy results, we would be wise to remember these words from Moses:

> Hear, O Israel: The LORD our God, the LORD is one. Love the LORD your God with all your heart and with all your soul and with all your strength. These commandments that I give you today are to be on your hearts. Impress them on your children. Talk about them when you sit at home and when you walk along the road, when you lie down and when you get up. Tie them as symbols on your hands and bind them on your foreheads. Write them on the doorframes of your houses and on your gates. (Deuteronomy 6:4-9)

Becoming an essential leader who shares the journey of youth ministry with other essential leaders doesn't happen overnight. It's not even something you can wrap up in nine months. But part of why we've given you extra ideas and your volunteers lots of extra space in their *Participant's Guides* is because we want you to keep these principles in your heart and to keep talking about them as you travel the road together to deep ministry.

The often-quoted (at least by me) philosopher Dallas Willard warns us in *The Divine Conspiracy*, "We are becoming who we will be—forever."[3] I want to become deep. And I want to share the ride with other leaders who are inviting teenagers to pursue an essential and ever-deepening intimacy with Jesus Christ.

ENDNOTES: INTRODUCTION

Welcome to the *Essential Leadership Leader's Guide*

1. Chap Clark and Kara Powell, *Deep Ministry in a Shallow World: Not-So-Secret Findings about Youth Ministry* (Grand Rapids: Youth Specialties/Zondervan, 2006).

2. Chap Clark and Kara Powell, *Deep Justice in a Broken World: Helping Your Kids Serve Others and Right the Wrongs Around Them* (Grand Rapids: Youth Specialties/Zondervan, 2007).

3. Dallas Willard, *The Divine Conspiracy: Rediscovering Our Hidden Life in God* (New York: HarperCollins, 1998), 11.

CHAPTER ONE

ESSENTIAL ASSESSMENT
A MAP THAT GETS OUR MINISTRY FROM HERE TO THERE

ESSENTIAL THOUGHTS[1]

Gather five youth workers, and you'll get five different opinions on which direction your ministry needs to head in the future. Gather five of your teenagers, and you'll have seven different opinions. Gather five parents of your teenagers, and you'll have 10 different opinions:

- More worship...
- No, less worship...
- More outreach...
- No way! We need more discipleship...
- More justice work and less small group time...
- Forget that. We need just the opposite...

In the midst of the conflicting opinions about what should be changed in your ministry, how can you make sure you and your team align yourselves with God's vision and not just whichever voice is shouting the loudest? How can you accurately assess your location today and discern the direction God is leading you tomorrow?

The good news is God is already at work in your ministry now and will be at work in the future. As Alan Roxburgh and Fred Romanuk remind us in *The Missional Leader*, "In what ways might God already be ahead of us and present among people in our community? How might we join with God in what is already happening?"[2]

One map that helps some youth ministries sense God's leading is an organizational leadership tool called the SWOT analysis. SWOT is an acronym for Strengths, Weaknesses, Opportunities, and Threats. SWOT isn't a new tool; in fact, it's been around for so long nobody really knows who invented it. Many people know what the SWOT analysis is. But in our experience few leaders understand what it does, and even fewer know how to use it as a map to experience essential leadership.

The Four Elements of SWOT

1. Strengths

Well-known leadership consultant Peter Drucker writes, "Most of us underestimate our own strengths. We take them for granted. What we are good at comes easy, and we believe that unless it comes hard, it can't be very good. As a result, we don't know our strengths, and we don't know how we can build on them."[3]

Accurately assessing our youth ministry's strengths can be difficult for a number of reasons. We may be in a setting that doesn't allow us to share such things, or we may not want to be perceived as arrogant or proud. As a result we either remain blind to those successes or keep them to ourselves. Because of this, many of us don't know what our ministry does well, what we should replicate, and what to celebrate with the rest of our team.

Identifying our strengths brings two primary benefits. First, we're immediately encouraged to repeat certain behaviors because they seem to produce the fruit we desire. Second, we see what we should be celebrating. Our team deserves the encouragement and the opportunity to see how our collective contributions are transforming kids.

Questions to help you understand your ministry's strengths:
> What are we doing well that we can thank God for?
> Whose contributions can we celebrate?
> What are we doing that's producing the outcomes we desire?
> What should we continue doing because we do it better than most?

2. Weaknesses

Unfortunately, in the same way we often don't take the time to identify our own strengths, we're also afraid to look at, much less articulate, the weaknesses of our ministry. As a result we rarely name and speak of things that aren't going well.

People seem to have this lingering fallacy that to acknowledge that something isn't working is to call into question the effectiveness of our entire ministry. But a call for continuous improvement is not a criticism of our work or calling. Instead it's an inherent part of our journey to essential leadership. As leadership guru Max De Pree reminds us, "The first responsibility of a leader is to define reality."[4] To look honestly at a situation and define reality is to speak the truth. It's not placing blame, not accusing anyone of wrongdoing—it's fulfilling the first responsibility of leadership.

Questions to help you understand your ministry's weaknesses:

> What's not working well?

> What can be improved?

> What needs to be removed altogether?

> What do we want to avoid in the future?

3. Opportunities

A friend of mine once described his ministry experience as more of a "here it comes, there it goes" cycle. He could envision what he wanted the ministry to look like. But more often than not, the ministry team was unable to hold onto the positive aspects of their work before they disappeared. The successes left as quickly as they came.

I would guess that many of us have experienced this dynamic to some degree, and we know how frustrating it can be when the *there it goes* occurs more frequently than the *here it comes.* But if we can identify the God-given opportunities brought before us, then we'll be able to choose the paths God is leading us toward instead of blindly racing—or even stumbling—past them.

Questions to help you understand your ministry's opportunities:

> What opportunities can we take better advantage of?

> What benefits can we leverage from the natural strengths of our ministry and community?

> What things outside our organization would help us achieve the results we're looking for?

4. Threats

Threats exist both outside and inside our ministries. Some are minor; some are imminently dangerous. They may be obvious (you have only one volunteer and she's moving away next month!), or they may be relatively hidden (your students' parents remain disconnected from youth ministry). We might be tempted initially to look past these threats; however, ignoring them generally doesn't make them disappear. On the contrary the longer threats are ignored, the more damaging they become. However, threats can be minimized—even neutralized—when we approach them honestly, directly, and thoughtfully.

SWOT Table

Specific Area of Ministry (If Any)	Strengths: What We Do Well	Weaknesses: What We Can Do Better	Opportunities: What We Can Leverage	Threats: What We Must Pay Attention To

Questions to help you understand your ministry's threats:

> To which threats must we pay attention?

> Which threats could potentially jeopardize our ministry efforts?

> What events happening in the world outside our church or ministry could potentially negatively affect our students or ministry and therefore need more attention and examination?

A hiker who actually cares about where he ends up would never check a map at the start of his trip and then never refer to it again. In the same way, no youth ministry team that wants to move from here to there does the SWOT analysis and then forgets about it. Keep your SWOT analysis in front of you. Review and prayerfully update it every three to six months. When you get to a fork in your youth ministry trail, this essential analysis might just show you which path to take.

SWOT Table

ESSENTIAL TEAM TALK

The Big Idea: Taking time to analyze our strengths, weaknesses, opportunities, and threats can help us follow the direction God has for our ministries.

You'll need—

> Three index cards on which you've written one of the following well-known leadership statements per card:

>> "IF YOU AIM AT NOTHING, YOU'LL HIT IT EVERYTIME." —UNKNOWN

>> "THE FIRST RESPONSIBILITY OF A LEADER IS TO DEFINE REALITY."
   —MAX DE PREE

>> "BEGIN WITH THE END IN MIND." —STEPHEN R. COVEY

> Four sheets of poster paper taped to a wall

> Two sheets of paper for each person

> Markers

> Crayons

> Tape

> An *Essential Leadership Participant's Guide* for each of your adult volunteers

> Have More Time? option: Copies of the blank SWOT table

Now

To launch into your discussion about essential assessment, hold up the three index cards while you explain, **On each of these cards, I've written a well-known leadership quote. Who wants to read one of these cards aloud?**

Distribute index cards to three different volunteers and then invite one of them to read the leadership statement aloud. When the first volunteer is finished, ask **How does this statement relate to essential leadership?**

Invite a second volunteer to read a quote aloud and ask the same question about its relevance to essential leadership. And you guessed what's next: Do the same process with the third volunteer.

Explain, **In these three quotes, we see the importance of both knowing where _we are_—our current reality—and knowing where we want _to head_—the end we're aiming for. Another way of thinking about where we're heading is to draw a picture of our preferred future.**

Distribute two pieces of paper and crayons to volunteers and ask them to write words or draw a picture on one piece of paper that depicts their description of the current reality of your youth ministry. On the second piece of paper, invite participants to write words or draw pictures to depict the direction they'd like your youth ministry to be heading.

When they're finished, invite them to share both pictures. Hang the current reality pictures on one wall of your meeting space and the where-we-want-to-be pictures on the opposite wall.

New

Point from the first wall to the second wall and explain, **It's no easy task getting from here to there. A SWOT analysis is one essential tool that can help us better determine where we are, as well as what steps we need to take to move forward.**

If you don't mind people throwing things at you, then you can add, **So let's take a swat at SWOT together.** (Sorry, we couldn't resist.)

Note: You can use SWOT to evaluate either your entire ministry or just a few portions of it, such as your small groups, your teaching, or your student leadership. Decide ahead of time what you need more of in your ministry and frame the rest of the discussion accordingly. You'll want to decide beforehand how much time you can spend on each of the four SWOT areas during your discussion and then stick to it. Otherwise it can be easy to let the conversation linger too long in one area. Either be the timekeeper yourself or assign someone to watch the clock and move the evaluation forward at the appropriate marks.

1. Strengths

Invite your leaders to turn to the New section in their *Essential Leadership Participant's Guide* and then ask, **Why is it good to identify our strengths?** After they've shared some answers, ask the first question the team can respond to in their journals (marked with a *Q:*).

Q: **So what do you think are our ministry's strengths?**

Label the first sheet of poster paper STRENGTHS and write your team's answers on it. If your group gets stuck before you've created a comprehensive list, ask one or more of these questions as a different way to trigger their thinking:

> **What are we doing well that we can thank God for?**
> **Whose contributions can we celebrate?**
> **What are we doing that's producing the outcomes we desire?**
> **What should we continue doing because we do it better than most?**

2. Weaknesses

Ask the following questions from the *Participant's Guide:*

Q: **What keeps us from identifying our weaknesses?**

Q: **What would we gain if we better identified our weaknesses?**

Q: **As we talk about our weaknesses together, what steps can we take to make sure no one, including me, ends up feeling blamed or attacked?**

If it would be helpful, explain that the healthiest youth ministries embrace a spirit of continuous improvement in which the leaders are constantly trying to learn and grow without blaming others for past or present mistakes. Then ask—

Q: **So what isn't working as well as we would hope?**

Move to the second poster paper, label it WEAKNESSES, and write your volunteers' answers on it. Again, if you need additional questions as conversation catalysts, try—

> What can be improved?
> What needs to be removed altogether?
> What do we want to avoid in the future?

Transition to the last two elements of the SWOT analysis by explaining: **The last two elements of the SWOT analysis refer to either opportunities or threats that often lie outside of our immediate ministry but impact us nonetheless.**

3. Opportunities

Begin with these questions:

Q: **What do we mean by opportunities?**

Q: **What are some of the opportunities our ministry can take advantage of?**

Move to the third poster paper, write OPPORTUNITIES on it, and jot down your volunteers' answers. Additional questions to help you think more broadly about opportunities include:

> **What benefits can we leverage from the natural strengths of our ministry and community?**
> **What things outside of our organization would help us achieve the results we're looking for?**

Have More Time?

Distribute copies of the blank SWOT table to your volunteers and ask them to list their own impressions of your ministry's strengths, weaknesses, opportunities, and threats before you discuss them as a large group. This will allow your leaders to generate their own ideas and not simply be swayed by what everyone else is saying. (Teenagers aren't the only ones who are influenced by the opinions of others!)

4. Threats

Start by asking—

> Q: **What happens if we ignore threats to our ministry?**

> Q: **So what might be some threats our ministry is facing now or might face in the near future?**

Write THREATS on the fourth piece of poster paper and list your volunteers' ideas. These additional questions might help your team if you get stuck:

> > **To which threats must we pay attention?**
> > **Which threats could potentially jeopardize our ministry efforts?**
> > **What events happening in the world outside our church or ministry could negatively affect our students or our ministry and therefore need more attention and examination?**

How

Review all four SWOT poster papers and ask: **Is there anything we can combine or delete because it seems redundant? Is there anything else we want to add?**

Make those changes on the four pieces of poster paper. Then ask—

> Q: **What themes do you see in what we've written?**

Explain, **Now I'm going to distribute a few markers and give you 16 votes, represented by 16 stars that you will each draw, to place in any of the four SWOT categories. But you can't exceed four votes in a category—that's the limit. These votes represent what you think is most important for us to focus on, either to fix or take advantage of, over the next six months.**

So to clarify, within each category, you can use four of your 16 votes however you'd like. You can give four separate items one vote each, two separate items two votes each, or one item all four votes. But again, don't exceed four votes in one category.

After you and your team members have finished voting, count up the stars next to each item and circle those items that received the most votes. Ask—

> Q: **What have we learned from our voting exercise?**

Q: **What in these voting results confirms what you would have guessed?**

Q: **What surprises you?**

Choose two to four items that received the most votes and invite your volunteers to get into different task forces to discuss these particular items. Give each task force 15 minutes to discuss the item and then have them report any initial recommended action steps they'd like to suggest. Encourage the groups to think about how students, volunteers, parents, or church members can contribute to that particular area so it doesn't end up being all the youth leader's job. These groups will only be able to scratch the surface in 15 minutes, but it's good to strike while the assessment iron is hot.

After the task forces have reported, either have them individually complete the Essential Assessment Action Plan at the end of Chapter One of their *Participant's Guide*, or you can complete it together as a large group based on ideas that emerged from all of the groups.

Close by asking each task force to huddle up and pray about the particular area—for God to give you a vision for how to get from here to there in such a way that honors God and deepens your ministry.

If it seems like a good physical reminder of your journey, start your prayer time standing on one side of the room to represent *here*—where we are now. Pray specifically about what's going well in your ministry today. Then walk together to the other side of the room to represent *there*—your goal or preferred future. Once you get *there*, ask God to bring about the changes to bring that vision to reality in your ministry.

ENDNOTES: CHAPTER ONE

Essential Assessment: A Map That Gets Our Ministry from Here to There

1. This section is adapted from an article entitled "Evaluation Part 1: Giving the Gift of Evaluation to Your Ministry" by Mark Maines, available at www.fulleryouthinstitute.org.

2. Alan J. Roxburgh and Fred Romanuk, *The Missional Leader: Equipping Your Church to Reach a Changing World* (San Francisco: Jossey-Bass, 2006), 24.

3. Peter F. Drucker, "Managing Knowledge Means Managing Oneself," *Leader to Leader*, no. 16 (Spring 2000), 8-10.

4. Max De Pree, *Leadership Is an Art* (New York: Doubleday, 1989), 9.

Essential Assessment Action Plan

Our team's ideas for how to move forward into essential assessment include:

OVERALL GOALS	ACTION STEPS TOWARD THESE GOALS	SPECIFIC PRAYER REQUESTS	SIGNS OF GOD'S ACTIVITY

CHAPTER TWO

ESSENTIAL MENTORS
EMPOWERING RELATIONSHIPS THAT WORK

ESSENTIAL THOUGHTS[1]

Wouldn't it be great to have the kind of mentoring Luke Skywalker had in the *Star Wars* trilogy? First, he had Obi-Wan Kenobi. Kenobi was instrumental in Luke's early lightsaber training and single-handedly freed Luke and his companions from certain death by sacrificing himself to Darth Vader. That's quite a mentor! Unfortunately, with Obi-Wan's final heroic act, he left Luke on his own to fight for truth, justice, and the Jedi way.

But then Luke ended up with Yoda as a mentor. One downside to Yoda's mentoring was that Luke had to carry him around on his back (but at least that made him portable). Yoda was constantly whispering all sorts of pithy phrases in Luke's ear. Granted, most of them were over Luke's head, at least at the time. But still, Luke was trained day and night by a wise Jedi Master whose 900 years of experience were unmatched in the galaxy.

One problem with the Skywalker-esque images of mentoring is that they set unrealistic expectations for the kind of mentoring we can generally expect in life outside the movies. Obi-Wan and Yoda were with Luke 24/7. They helped him with everything from lifting starfighters out of swamps to challenges of the will and body. These days few people can give that kind of time or have that kind of power. (Or for that matter, how many mentors are the size of Yoda and can fit inside a backpack that you wear throughout the day?)

In youth and family ministry we have a shortage of such be-all, end-all mentors. Youth workers who are looking for someone to help them be better leaders, spouses, parents, friends, and followers of Christ often become frustrated when no Yoda drifts into their lives and promises to "make you a better person, I will."

In his study of the development of leaders, Robert ("Bobby") Clinton from Fuller Theological Seminary has created a paradigm to help leaders receive mentoring even when there aren't enough mentors to go around. Instead of expecting one perfect, all-encompassing mentor, Clinton recommends developing a constellation of mentors—a small galaxy perhaps—none of whom is perfect, but all of whom can speak into your life.

In his work with Paul D. Stanley, Clinton has divided the ideal mentor into mentoring functions. As youth workers we can almost always find someone who can do one or more of these functions. By picturing the mentoring you need along a continuum of intensity, you'll have a better chance of getting the mentoring you need.[2]

According to Clinton, at the far left side of the diagram is the *discipler*. A discipler is someone who empowers you in the basics of following Christ. Often this type of mentoring is crucial when someone is beginning to develop his or her relationship with Christ.

The second type of mentor is a bit less intensive and is called a *spiritual guide*. A spiritual guide provides accountability, direction, and insight that lead to greater spiritual maturity. Often called a *spiritual director*, this type of mentor has gained popularity in recent years.

The third type of mentor, the *counselor*, is still less intensive. This person provides critical advice and perspectives to help you navigate your life and ministry circumstances. At times this may come through professional therapy, but it can also come from close friends or accountability relationships.

The fourth type of mentor is a *coach*. A coach gives you the motivation, skills, and application needed to meet a task or challenge. Common examples of coaches in youth ministry include those who help you develop your speaking skills, your counseling abilities, or your small-group facilitation skills.

Clinton labels a fifth type of mentor as a *sponsor*. This person provides career guidance and protection, as well as networking opportunities, as you move through a ministry or organization. He might open the door for a promotion or for a new ministry opportunity you wouldn't get otherwise.

The final and least deliberate type of mentor is a model. A *model* can be either a contemporary, living example you want to emulate or a historical example of a leader who inspires your life and ministry. This final category allows youth workers in any context to receive mentoring by studying the lives of previous leaders or reading provocative autobiographies and biographies.

Given these different types of mentors, when you're in search of one, it's wise to:

1. Consider the areas of your life or ministry in which you need or desire mentoring.

2. Ask yourself what type(s) of mentoring best corresponds with those areas.

3. Brainstorm a person(s) you know who might fit the type of mentor you've identified for yourself.

4. If applicable, prayerfully ask that person(s) to mentor you, making sure you clearly spell out the type of mentoring you're hoping to receive. If the mentoring or mentoring relationship is less deliberate (meaning you won't need to ask the person(s) for an official "mentoring relationship"), be sure to design an intentional plan so you get the consistent input you need.

5. Evaluate the mentoring relationship approximately every three months to make sure the relationship keeps growing and improving.

Maybe you'll never find the perfect Yoda to accompany you on every leg of your journey. But maybe you don't have to. By using the mentoring continuum, it's possible for you to piece together your own Yoda network in order to get the essential mentoring you need (lightsaber not included).

ESSENTIAL TEAM TALK

The Big Idea: We can both be mentored and mentor students more effectively with whatever time and energy we have.

You'll need—

> A copy of the DVD *Hitch* (Columbia Pictures, 2005) and a way to play a movie clip (a video projector, computer, or TV plus a DVD player)

> A whiteboard

> Markers

> Have More Time? option: Two pieces of paper, two stamps, and two envelopes for each volunteer

> Pens

> Bibles

> An *Essential Leadership Participant's Guide* for each of your adult volunteers

Now

Greet your volunteers and touch base on the action plan your team developed during your previous team meeting(s). Celebrate what God and your team have done and pinpoint future next steps.

Next explain: **Today we're going to talk about another essential part of youth ministry leadership: Mentoring. We're going to begin by looking at a movie clip that helps us think about good mentoring, as well as not-so-good mentoring.**

Play the scene from *Hitch*, chapter 15, called "The Fire and the Pizza" (approximately 49:30 into the movie), which starts when Hitch (played by Will Smith) says, "Now about the DJ...generally I have a firm no-dancing policy." The clip ends at 52:05 when Will Smith says, "Get out," and slaps Albert Brennaman (played by Kevin James).

Play the DVD and then ask, **What was good about the mentoring relationship between Hitch and Albert? What was not so good? How would you define *mentoring*?** Write their answers on the whiteboard.

Ask your staff to turn to the Essential Team Talk section of their *Participant's Guide* and then continue:

These are all great definitions of *mentoring*.

However, for the purposes of our discussion today, we're going to define mentoring as: *Empowering another person* toward *God's purposes*.[3] **What words stand out to you in that definition?**

Let's think about the mentoring relationships already in our lives. Please return to your *Participant's Guide*. I'm going to give you a few minutes to write down—

1. The list of people you're currently mentoring in some way.

2. The list of people you'd like to mentor.

3. The list of people who are mentoring you in some way.

4. The list of people you would like to be mentoring you.

When they have finished their lists, continue by asking—

Q: **When we look at these lists, what do most of us feel?**

After team members share some answers, continue by sharing—**GUILT. We feel guilty either because we have so many people on our lists that we aren't doing a very good job with those relationships or because we have so few people on our lists that we wonder if we're really investing enough in other people.**

Today we're going to learn how to replace this guilt with a sense of freedom and joy. We're also going to gain tools that will help us mentor and be mentored with whatever energy and time we have.

New

Continue: **Much of our guilt stems from our false belief that mentors are be-all and end-all influences on us. We tend to think of mentoring as if we were Luke Skywalker from the *Star Wars* series and the type of mentor we need is Yoda.**

One problem with this Skywalker-esque image of mentoring is that it creates unrealistic expectations for the kind of mentoring we can generally expect in life outside the movies. Yoda was with Luke 24/7. Yoda helped him with everything from lifting starfighters out of swamps to challenges of the will and body. These days few people can give that kind of time or have that kind of power. (For that matter, how many mentors are the size of Yoda and can fit inside a backpack that you wear throughout the day?)

Have More Time?

To help your leaders recognize the constellation of mentors who have already shaped them, invite them to make a list of people who have already empowered them by having them answer these questions:

1. Who taught you to ride a bike?

2. Who trained you at your first job?

3. Who taught you to drive a car?

4. What neighbors, friends, or family members did you admire as a child?

5. In your initial steps of faith, which teachers, church leaders, or pastors first shaped your view of Jesus?

6. Which teachers or leaders have shaped your view of Jesus more recently?

7. Which books or articles have you read in the last few years that have impacted you (other than *Essential Leadership* and the *Essential Leadership Participant's Guide*, of course)?

8. As you were growing up, which teachers helped sharpen your abilities to think and to communicate your thoughts?

9. What is a special skill you have? Who helped you develop that skill?

When your group has finished, ask—**What does this list tell you about the mentors in your life?**

As a result we who are looking for someone to help us be better ministers, spouses, parents, friends, and followers of Christ often become frustrated when no Yoda drifts into our lives and promises to "make you a better person, I will."

Continue with—**According to research conducted by Dr. Bobby Clinton at Fuller Seminary, there are different types of mentoring relationships that fall along a continuum of intensity. We'll start by discussing the most intense type of mentoring relationships and end with the least intense.**

The Mentoring Continuum

As you walk through these six types of mentors, try to give examples of these types from your own life or of a time when you were this type of mentor in a student's life. If you can't think of any examples from your own experience, feel free to point out examples of the ways your adult leaders are mentoring along the continuum and invite them to identify mentoring relationships as well.

The following continuum depicts the intensity continuum and the locations of the six types of mentoring along that continuum.[4]

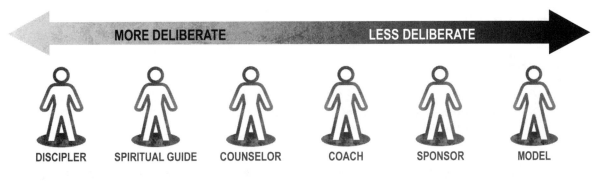

MORE DELIBERATE   LESS DELIBERATE

DISCIPLER   SPIRITUAL GUIDE   COUNSELOR   COACH   SPONSOR   MODEL

1. **Discipler: Empowers in _all_ areas of life. A discipler is a very traditional and intensive form of mentoring. Usually a discipler invests holistically in your life and ministry several hours a week.**

2. **Spiritual Guide: Empowers by helping with _decisions_ and _disciplines_ that produce greater spiritual maturity. A spiritual guide, also known as a spiritual director, tends to focus primarily on the spiritual aspects of your life. In some cases, this could also be a small group leader.**

3. **Counselor: Empowers through _advice_ and _perspective_ on important areas of your life, your relationships, and your ministry. A counselor usually has the ability to ask insightful questions and often plays a role of accountability in your life.**

4. **Coach: Empowers through _motivation_ and _skill development_ in the face of new or challenging tasks. A coach helps you with a specific skill you're growing in or an event or project you're developing. Since the tasks you face are likely constantly changing, this person might be your cheerleader and trainer for only a season.**

5. **Sponsor: Empowers through _guidance_, often in your work environment. A sponsor provides insight and advice to help you in your professional life.**

6. **Model: Empowers by being an example that _inspires_ and _teaches_. This person is someone you've modeled your life around because of your admiration of her. This could be someone who has already passed on or someone you don't know personally (such as an author or a speaker).**

Now ask—

Q: **How does this continuum help you think about mentoring in new ways?**

Q: **Earlier we agreed that we often feel guilty when we think about mentoring. How does thinking about mentoring along this continuum make you feel now?**

How

Invite your adult leaders to turn to the How section in their *Participant's Guide* and answer the following questions:

Mentors for you

Q: **What are your primary needs for mentoring right now?**

Q: **Given these needs, what type(s) of mentor is most important for you? Circle that type(s) in the following continuum.**

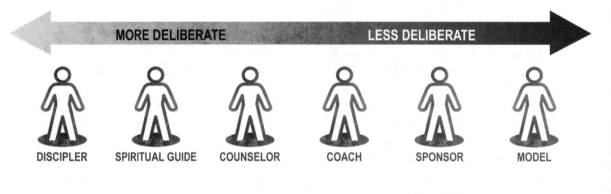

MORE DELIBERATE   LESS DELIBERATE

DISCIPLER   SPIRITUAL GUIDE   COUNSELOR   COACH   SPONSOR   MODEL

Q: **Who might be able to be this type of mentor to you?**

Q: **What do you have to gain by asking this person to be your mentor? What might you lose?**

Students you mentor

Transition to reflecting about relationships with students by moving to the next block of questions in the journal. Say—**Now let's think about the students we're trying to empower.**

Q: What students are you mentoring at various points along the mentoring continuum? Go ahead and write their names at the appropriate points on the continuum in your journal.

MORE DELIBERATE   LESS DELIBERATE

DISCIPLER   SPIRITUAL GUIDE   COUNSELOR   COACH   SPONSOR   MODEL

Q: What does this tell you about how you're mentoring right now? What's good about that? What might be problematic about that?

Q: Given this, what might you want to do differently?

Q: What can we do on this team to support each other as we try to mentor students along this continuum?

Have More Time?

Distribute a pen and two pieces of note paper to each of your adult volunteers. Give them a few minutes to write two brief notes of affirmation—one to a mentor who has empowered them in the past or present and a second to someone they're trying to mentor right now. When everyone is finished, distribute envelopes and stamps. If your staff members have addresses with them, offer to collect the sealed letters and mail them the next day. If the staff don't have the relevant addresses with them, encourage them to take the notes, envelopes, and stamps home to mail in the next few days.

Try to help your leaders come up with specific ideas. And if you're comfortable, ask them what you can personally do to support their mentoring relationships. You may even want to take time to identify students who need specific types of mentoring relationships, then brainstorm ideas of adults in your congregation or community who could potentially provide that mentoring. That way you and your team begin to envision a constellation of mentors around each student and leader in your ministry.

Invite your leaders to turn to the Essential Mentoring Action Plan in their *Participant's Guides* and use its rows as a way to pinpoint specific goals, action steps, and prayer requests.

Close by reading Proverbs 13:20: **"Walk with the wise and become wise, for a companion of fools suffers harm."** Read Proverbs 13:20 one more time and invite your volunteers to meditate quietly for a few moments on the imagery of walking with the wise. Read the same verse a third time, and invite your staff to pray silently for the students in your ministry—that they would be surrounded by wise friends and adults, including yourselves. Encourage your staff to pray that God would provide a constellation of mentors for your students, all of whom would help your students gain essential wisdom.

ENDNOTES: CHAPTER TWO

Essential Mentors: Empowering Relationships That Work

1. This section is adapted from an article entitled "Getting the Mentoring You Need" by Kara Powell, available at www.fulleryouthinstitute.org.

2. Adapted from J. Robert Clinton and Paul D. Stanley, *Connecting: The Mentoring Relationships You Need to Succeed in Life* (Colorado Springs, Colo.: NavPress, 1992), 41.

3. Ibid., 38.

4. Ibid., 41.

Essential Mentoring Action Plan

Our team's ideas for how to move forward into essential mentoring include:

OVERALL GOALS	ACTION STEPS TOWARD THESE GOALS	SPECIFIC PRAYER REQUESTS	SIGNS OF GOD'S ACTIVITY

CHAPTER THREE

ESSENTIAL HEALING
HELPING KIDS, FAMILIES, AND COMMUNITIES TOWARD GOOD GRIEF

ESSENTIAL THOUGHTS[1]

"Grieve now or regret it later."

That was the most common advice people gave a friend of mine when she lost her father at the age of 20. She wanted to heed their warnings, but she had only one problem: She didn't know how to grieve. She remembers sitting in her room and staring at pictures, trying to stir up emotions and thinking, *Am I doing it? Am I grieving?*

Knowing how to grieve well and support students in their pain may be one of the most valuable resources we can gain in our journey toward essential leadership. When we're unsure about how to respond to grief, our students may feel a subtle pressure to "get over it" or to deal with their losses by themselves. When we're comfortable with grief, our students will be more likely to talk to us about their pain and find their own good grief.

When Do We Need to Grieve?

Of course we all know grief is an inevitable part of life. But to the surprise of many, grief doesn't just occur when someone dies. In *All Our Losses, All Our Griefs*, authors Kenneth Mitchell and Herbert Anderson emphasize that *any loss* experienced must be grieved.

They divide loss into six categories:[2]

- Material Loss: "Yes, you can grieve if you lose your cell phone."

- Relationship Loss: "Yes, you can grieve if you break up with your boyfriend."

- Intrapsychic Loss (or "loss of a dream"): "Yes, you can grieve not getting the job you wanted."

- Functional Loss: "Yes, you can grieve breaking your arm."

- Role Loss: "Yes, you can grieve being single if you get married."

- Systemic Loss: "Yes, you can grieve if your child leaves home and the family dynamics change."

How to Support a Student Toward Good Grief

There are different ways to support students when they initially experience a loss and continue to work through the grief process. When a kid or adult first experiences loss, keep the following in mind:

1. Avoid asking probing questions that hurt. Often our words to kids and families who are grieving bring more pain than comfort. After "I'm sorry," we often ask questions such as—

> Was she sick for a long time?

> Was the accident his fault?

> Was she a Christian?

> Were you close?

These questions themselves aren't harmful, but sometimes the reason we ask them isn't out of concern. We ask because we don't know what to say next. Instead, try inviting students to share rather than investigating. This means being observant, taking cues about how much the person wants to share, and offering to listen if he or she wants to divulge more.

2. Be careful not to compare, which we're prone to do. Using ourselves as the reference point, we tend to use a subtle scale from "not as bad as" to "worse than" us. In *A Grace Disguised*, Jerry Sittser explains that when we compare, we are driven to one of two unhealthy extremes. Those who have been determined to have a loss that's "not that bad" feel as if their loss isn't valid and has been "dismissed as unworthy of attention and recognition."[3] On the other end of the spectrum, those who have a loss deemed as "worse than" often convince themselves they're alone in their suffering and that no one can understand or help.

3. Be present and silent. Overwhelmingly, the research and literature on grieving suggest that the most helpful way to support people is to be present with them silently. Mitchell and Anderson write, "Two warring needs develop: the need to be alone with one's grief and the need not to be isolated from meaningful communities of support."[4] They describe a beautiful

Jewish custom called "sitting *shiva*" (pronounced "shee-vah") in which friends and family come and sit with the bereaved person at his home for seven days, but without saying anything except maybe hello, good-bye, or *shalom*. How wonderful if we practiced that today! It would eliminate all the awkward "I'm sorrys," the fumbling over words, and the feeble attempts to answer all of the *why* questions. (Another great description of this Jewish process and its contributions to healing is found in *Mudhouse Sabbath* by Lauren Winner.)

This is good news for us as we support others who are in pain. Often our best response is to be present, which frees us from feeling as if we need to fix the situation. Mitchell and Anderson note, "It is equally important to demonstrate God's suffering love by our willingness to listen to suffering and grief, and not give in to the impulse to run from the pain, shut off the complaint, or respond too quickly with pious platitudes," all of which can be symptomatic of our failure to deal with our own past and present pain.[5]

The Two Time Frames of Good Grief

The research on loss suggests that a successful grieving process involves two time frames: Remembering the past and hoping for the future.[6]

Remembering the past

When grieving a death or a loss, it's important to remember the actual person or situation for who he was or what it was in your life, complete with strengths, weaknesses, and quirks. When remembering, people can sometimes focus on all the good or all the bad parts, but both are important.

As youth workers we have opportunities to encourage this type of holistic remembering. For example, if a class of seniors is about to graduate, it isn't uncommon to have a time of acknowledgment or reflection. During this exciting time remembering can sometimes be filled with good memories and testimonies of growth. But for at least some students, if not all, we may also need to acknowledge a darker side.

Hoping for the future

While one aspect of the grief process is the ability to look into the past, the other side is the ability to look to the future and hope again. To hope we must be able to look ahead and envision a new life. For some students this may look like dreaming about long-range plans, while for others it's waking up and making a plan for the day.

As youth workers we can help foster this "re-dreaming" process. For example, the loss of a friend (whether the friend drifted away, moved away, or passed away) is devastating for teens.

Coupled with the loss of the friend is also the loss of any plans made together. It can sometimes feel disloyal to make new plans or continue on without the friend, but we can walk alongside students to help brainstorm and encourage them in this process. When students can hope again, when they can make new connections and have new dreams, it's a sign that they're experiencing good grief.[7]

Where Is God in Grief? The Role of Lament

Asking why God would allow loss—and even where God is in the midst of pain—might seem a necessary evil in the midst of students' process to good grief. In reality, creating space for those types of questions is an important part of our worship and discipleship with individual students, as well as our entire youth ministry.

Theologian Walter Brueggemann challenges the church to reconsider lament as a category of worship we've mostly forgotten or avoided. Lament consists of crying out to God—even *complaining* to God—in the full expression of our pain and doubt. Though this can be pretty messy, the book of Psalms actually contains a full 65 laments for us to see and sometimes use as models.

Brueggemann calls these *psalms of disorientation*. He urges that our worship in community with others shouldn't just focus on the cheerful aspects of life and faith, but must also consider the disturbingly incoherent and painful realities as well.[8]

Brueggemann warns,

> Where the capacity to initiate lament is absent, one is left only with praise and doxology. God then is omnipotent, always to be praised. The believer is nothing, and can praise or accept guilt uncritically where life with God does not function properly. The outcome is a "False Self," bad faith that is based in fear and guilt and lived out as resentful or self-deceptive works of righteousness. The absence of lament makes a religion of coercive obedience the only possibility.[9]

Incorporating lament into our ministries takes careful thought, but it doesn't have to be elaborate. Perhaps you could start by taking time in your next worship service for a reading of a psalm that doesn't end with a sense of hopefulness, such as Psalms 10, 61, 80, or 88. Ask a couple of reflection questions such as, "Is it okay to say these kinds of things to God? How do you think it might deepen your relationship with God? Where could this kind of prayer go from here?" Then read through the psalm again and invite students to journal or draw their own continuing prayer for a few minutes. Afterward talk through their feelings of comfort or discomfort in approaching God that way. Additional individual laments you could use are Psalms 6, 39, 102, 109, or 142. After going through these psalms of lament, you could contrast the attitude of despair and questioning with the confidence of Psalms 27 or 46.

As youth workers we may fear taking students to those places of doubt, anger, and disappointment with God. We sometimes short-cut the process by "fixing" their doubts, instead of listening when our students venture to explore those feelings. However, failing to create an environment for authentic lament can result in spiritually and psychologically short-circuiting the necessary healing process.

Authentic trust in God may take a long time, and teenagers need faithful adults to journey that difficult road with them. We in youth ministry have the opportunity to offer students the hope of Christ and his *reorienting power* and grace that lead to good grief.

ESSENTIAL TEAM TALK

The Big Idea: As kids inevitably experience loss, we can be a resource to help them deal with—and even grow in the midst of—their pain.

You'll need—

> Canned drinks for all of your volunteers

> A hammer

> A picture of yourself as a teenager

> A whiteboard

> Markers

> Optional: Encourage volunteers to bring a picture of themselves as teenagers

> An *Essential Leadership Participant's Guide* for each of your volunteers

Now

Distribute the canned drinks to your staff as a special treat and touch base on the action plan your team developed during your previous team meeting(s). Celebrate what God and your team have done and pinpoint future next steps.

To transition to the topic of deep hurt and essential healing, show your leaders a picture of you as a teenager. If you encouraged your volunteers to bring in pictures of themselves, then have them share those as well. Once the laughter and mockery subside, share about the pain you experienced as a teenager. If possible share one or two sources of relatively minor pain (*I thought I wasn't going to have a date for my senior prom*) and one or two sources of relatively major pain (*My stepdad worked so much I felt like I didn't have a dad*).

Invite your volunteers to turn to the Now section in their *Participant's Guide* and then ask—

Q: **When it comes to teenagers, in what ways is their pain connected to loss?**

Q: **What were some of the relatively minor sources of pain you experienced when you were a teenager?**

Q: **What were some of the more major sources of pain or loss that hurt you as a teenager?**

Q: **In what ways did that pain affect you negatively?**

Q: **In what ways did that pain or loss become a source of growth or something re-deemed for God's purposes?**

Q: **How are the sources of pain, both major and minor, that we faced as teenagers similar to those faced by the students in our ministry and community today?**

Separate your leaders into smaller teams. Invite a volunteer to read aloud the six types of loss described by Kenneth Mitchell and Herbert Anderson in *All Our Losses, All Our Griefs* and listed in the following Our Students' Losses table.[10] (It's also in their *Participant's Guide*.)

Our Students' Losses

TYPE OF LOSS	EXAMPLES IN OUR STUDENTS
Material Loss: "I lost my cell phone."	
Relationship Loss: "I lost my girlfriend."	
Intrapsychic Loss (or "Loss of a Dream"): "I didn't get into the college I dreamed of attending" or "I didn't make it to the next round of drama auditions."	
Functional Loss: "My car doesn't start."	
Role Loss: "My stepmom just had a baby, so now I'm not the youngest anymore."	
Systemic Loss: "My older sister just moved into an apartment, so it's like she's not a part of our family anymore."	

Now say, **Together with your team, come up with real-life examples of the six types of loss and list them in the right column, making sure to maintain student anonymity as appropriate. What effects do these losses have on our kids?**

To illustrate the idea that the same painful events affect different students in different ways, get out your hammer and grab two empty soda cans from your now-less-thirsty volunteers. Ask a volunteer to think about a student she knows and—without mentioning the name—invite her to share a way the student has experienced loss. At that point explain that the hammer represents the difficult event. The first soda can represents a student who has experienced that loss. Use the hammer to dent the first can just a bit.

Next, explain that the second can represents a second student who experienced the same type of loss but feels it more dramatically. At this point use your hammer to dent the second can more severely. You could even be pretty dramatic and place the can on the floor and hammer it until it's smashed.

Ask—**What do you think makes a difference in how these two different students respond to the same type of loss?** (The research-based answer is that they have different coping strategies.)

New

At this point draw the following diagram on the whiteboard.[11] Invite your group to turn to the New section in their *Participant's Guides* and fill in their blank diagrams.

Tell the group: **As you can see in the diagram, teenagers' coping strategies in response to difficult events determine whether their pain is increased or decreased.**

Q: **What coping strategies have you seen our students use effectively to reduce pain?**

Q: **What coping strategies don't seem to decrease pain?**

Explain: **The good news is that while we can't always control teens' painful events, we can give them improved strategies to help them cope better.**

How

Continue: **So if we stopped this discussion right now, it'd be pretty depressing. But the good news is—there's a paradigm called the Three Rs that we can use to give teenagers the coping strategies they need in the midst of more severe losses, ones in which they've truly been traumatized. Although these Three Rs were developed based on research done with victims of abuse, they can also help our students who have been traumatized in other ways learn how to cope. The healthiest coping strategies will help teenagers explore their emotions and respond actively to their difficulties. The Three Rs make progress in both areas.**

At this point, walk through this list of the Three Rs with your volunteers, highlighting particular points and even including illustrations from your own conversations with students (keeping the students anonymous).

1. Reassurance

> **The student's feelings are _normal_.**
> **He is _not to blame_ for whatever trauma occurred.**
> **Point out her _strengths_; boost her self-esteem. Tell her how proud of her you are for having the courage to talk to you.**
> **Encourage him that his feelings will likely get easier to handle over time.**

2. Retelling

> **Provide a safe place for the student to tell her story.**
> **_Listen_ and _support_ him when he retells the story.**
>   • **The story may unfold over time.**
>   • **Be patient as new details come out.**
>   • **Allow students to talk at their own pace.**

Explain: **Being with a teen in the midst of this retelling process is one of the most important gifts you can give to him or her. Students can feel completely alone after a painful or traumatic event, so for them to reach out and feel heard is a huge step in healing.**

Where Can You Go to Get Answers to Your Questions About Abuse Reporting?

> Supervisors: See if your student ministry leader, church education director, or senior pastor has some sort of policy in place that you should follow.

> Department of Child and Family Services: You can call anonymously and ask questions about particular situations to find out their recommendations and whether or not it's a situation you're mandated to report.

> Child Abuse Prevention Council:
  http://www.capcsac.org/childabuse/laws.html

> Child Welfare Information Gateway:
  http://www.childwelfare.gov/responding/mandated.cfm

3. Resources

> Create a _safety plan_ and help the student find safe places (meaning actual physical locations) to go when he or she feels threatened or scared.

> Brainstorm some _safe and nonjudgmental_ people the student can trust.

> Find ways to have _fun_ with her!

> Get _professionals_ involved if...

  • Abuse is currently happening, or the student is still in danger.

  • The student talks about hurting someone or hurting himself.

  • The student doesn't feel better over time.

  • You feel overwhelmed.

As you talk with your team about getting help from professionals, identify the resources that are available either within or through your church. Include local therapists and youth experts, especially those who charge reasonable fees or do pro-bono work.

> Commit the student to God through regular _prayer_.

> Remember that a teenager often shows his hurt by _acting out_. So be consistent with consequences, but remember that pain or trauma might lie behind his poor choices.

Conclude by walking through the following "How Would You Respond If a Hurting Kid Said…" quotations. (They're also in the *Participant's Guide*.) After each case study, invite your volunteers to share their ideas before sharing or paraphrasing from the tips that follow.

How would you respond if a hurting kid said…?

"No matter what I tell you, will you promise to keep it confidential?"

Affirm the student's desire to confide very personal information with you, but let her know that in some cases you are required by law to take action in certain ways (find out what your state, local, and church laws and policies mandate). Many times youth workers are required to break confidentiality if a minor is planning self-harm or harm to others or is currently experiencing abuse of some kind. So answer the question by saying, "I will as long as someone—including you—won't be hurt if I do."

"All things work together for good, so God must have a plan."

Ask the student where he's heard that before. If you have a Bible handy, turn to Romans 8:28 and read it together.

Emphasize the role of fallenness, sin, and evil in the world (your own ministry might have a particular nuance on this, of course) as the source of much of our pain and brokenness. Help the student look for the distinction between God as *initiator* of pain and God as *redeemer* of pain. In other words, does God's promise to use pain for bringing about good mean that God causes traumatic events in our lives?

Make sure students don't try to deny their own pain because "God has a plan."

"If I prayed more or had real enough faith, this wouldn't have happened."

Overtly or covertly, we tend to spread this misperception of what prayer is supposed to accomplish. Too often ministries teach some version of God-as-wish-granter and make prayer our tool of manipulation to command God to do what we want. While faith is part of how God sometimes works, there is no simple equation to guarantee that *enough faith = God answers our prayers as we want him to*. Interestingly, in Matthew 9:2 and 9:22, faith seems to be a factor in Jesus' healings, but in Matthew 8:26, Jesus calms the storm despite the disciples' lack of faith.

"A God who is really good wouldn't have let this happen to me."

Wrestle together—maybe even using Psalms of lament—with how God can be faithful and good, yet also allow such great evil and pain to exist in our lives. Probably the most important thing you can do is reassure a student she's not alone and encourage her to keep asking questions and seeking God.

But don't try to resolve this one. It's one of the most difficult questions of faith, and it's important for all of us to wrestle with it. For some practical tips in dealing with this issue, check out an excellent article called "Your Pain: Six Lenses to Help" by Jude Tiersma Watson. You can find it on the Fuller Youth Institute Web site at www.fulleryouthinstitute.org/2009/03/your-pain/.

"It hurts so much—I don't know if I'll ever feel better again."

Reassure him that while the pain feels—and probably is—unbearable right now, it will likely get better over time. And unfortunately, it might get worse before it gets better. Encourage him that slowly he'll begin to feel more able to cope with everyday life again. Prod him to use as many resources as he has available to him in the meantime to help him get through each day. Encourage him to see a therapist if the pain remains unbearable.

"Other people go through things way worse than this, so I'm actually pretty lucky."

Help her to be careful not to minimize her own pain. While it's helpful to put loss in perspective when we think about the things other people lose, it sometimes makes us feel guilty or weak for feeling so sad and overwhelmed by our own loss. Each loss needs to be recognized for what it is: A very real loss to be grieved. And grief is always painful in some way.

Invite your leaders to turn to the Essential Healing Action Plan in their *Participant's Guide* and use its rows as a way to pinpoint specific goals, action steps, and prayer requests.

Next invite one of your volunteers to read aloud Psalm 88, which appears in their *Participant's Guide.*

> LORD, you are the God who saves me; day and night I cry out to you. May my prayer come before you; turn your ear to my cry. I am overwhelmed with troubles and my life draws near to death. I am counted among those who go down to the pit; I am like one without strength.
>
> I am set apart with the dead, like the slain who lie in the grave, whom you remember no more, who are cut off from your care. You have put me in the lowest pit, in the darkest depths. Your wrath lies heavily on me; you have overwhelmed me with all your waves. You have taken from me my closest friends and have made me repulsive to them. I am confined and cannot escape; my eyes are dim with grief.
>
> I call to you, LORD, every day; I spread out my hands to you. Do you show your wonders to the dead? Do their spirits rise up and praise you? Is your love declared in the grave, your faithfulness in Destruction? Are your wonders known in the place of darkness, or your righteous deeds in the land of oblivion?

Essential Healing Action Plan

Our team's ideas for how to care for students who've been deeply hurt include:

OVERALL GOALS	ACTION STEPS TOWARD THESE GOALS	SPECIFIC PRAYER REQUESTS	SIGNS OF GOD'S ACTIVITY

But I cry to you for help, LORD; in the morning my prayer comes before you. Why, LORD, do you reject me and hide your face from me? From my youth I have suffered and been close to death; I have borne your terrors and am in despair. Your wrath has swept over me; your terrors have destroyed me. All day long they surround me like a flood; they have completely engulfed me. You have taken from me friend and neighbor—darkness is my closest friend. (Psalm 88)

Close by silently praying together as a team, using the following prayer prompts. Pause for a few moments after every prayer prompt, but make sure your volunteers pray silently so students' pain is kept appropriately confidential.

- God, today I'm thinking of a hurting student named...
- In the midst of the pain, please help this student to follow the example of Psalm 88 and call out to you because...
- Please show me how to...
- Help our ministry to be a place where...
- Thank you for being a God who...

ENDNOTES: CHAPTER THREE

Essential Healing: Helping Kids, Families, and Communities Toward Good Grief

1. This section is adapted from two articles entitled "Good Grief" by Kimberly Williams and "In the Aftermath: Processing Trauma Through the Lens of Lament" by Brad Griffin and Cynthia Eriksson, available at www.fulleryouthinstitute.org, as well as materials and consultation provided by the Headington Program at Fuller Seminary. "In the Aftermath" was also published in the May/June 2006 issue of *The Journal of Student Ministries*, © DevelopMinistries, www.developministries.com. Used with permission.

   The Headington Program conducts innovative research in order to better understand the variables affecting acute, chronic, and post-traumatic stress and creatively applies this knowledge to the development of better methods of identification and treatment of individuals, families, and communities that have been affected by chronic stress and trauma.

2. Kenneth R. Mitchell and Herbert Anderson, *All Our Losses, All Our Griefs: Resources for Pastoral Care* (Louisville, Ky.: Westminster John Knox Press, 1983), 36-46.

3. Jerry Sittser, *A Grace Disguised: How the Soul Grows through Loss* (Grand Rapids, Mich.: Zondervan, 1995), 29.

4. Mitchell and Anderson, 67.

5. Ibid., 138.

6. Two of the most helpful resources in developing this have been Jerry Sittser's chapter on "Forgive and Remember" in *A Grace Disguised* and the four tasks of mourning described in J. William Worden's *Grief Counseling and Grief Therapy: A Handbook for the Mental Health Practitioner*, third ed. (New York: Springer Publishing, 2002), 27-37.

7. This is not to suggest that the goal of good grief is to help students move on and not think about the friendship lost. Some research suggests that children who move on in new relationships but periodically imagine what their deceased parent would say or do in response to their circumstances are actually healthier than those who don't. See Phyllis R. Silverman, Steven Nickman, and J. William Worden, "Detachment Revisited: The Child's Reconstruction of a Dead Parent," *American Journal of Orthopsychiatry* 62, no. 4 (October 1992), 494-503.

8. Walter Brueggemann, *The Message of the Psalms: A Theological Commentary* (Minneapolis, Minn.: Augsburg Old Testament Studies, 1984), 51.

9. Walter Brueggemann, *The Psalms and the Life of Faith*, ed. Patrick D. Miller (Minneapolis, Minn.: Augsburg Fortress, 1995), 103-104.

10. Mitchell and Anderson, 36-46.

11. This diagram is based upon the theories of Richard S. Lazarus and Susan Folkman, *Stress, Appraisal, and Coping* (New York: Springer Publishing, 1984). An important phase not shown in the diagram is teenagers' appraisal of the seriousness of the threat, as well as their appraisal of the resilience of their resources and coping strategies.

CHAPTER FOUR

ESSENTIAL JUSTICE
MOVING BEYOND THE NEWS CRAWL

ESSENTIAL THOUGHTS[1]

Will anyone who feels a love-hate relationship with the infamous CNN news crawl please step forward?

Good. I'm glad I'm not alone.

In the midst of our hectic ministry schedules, sometimes news sound bites are all we have time for. The Middle East still has problems. Got it. Bipartisan bickering continues on Capitol Hill. Bummer, but not much I can do about it. The Hollywood celeb of the week has started a new environmental campaign. Great, I can use that as an illustration in Sunday's talk.

While we're not getting the fine print, at least we're getting the headlines. Isn't hearing about the news of the world for a few seconds better than not hearing about it at all?

Maybe, but maybe not.

Sure, we're all a bit better informed thanks to the news crawl. But isn't it possible that these bite-sized nuggets serve as some sort of placebo—making us (and our students) think we're interacting with world events when, in reality, we forget and move on as quickly as the next headline scrolls across the screen?

I wonder if the same dynamics are being replicated in the service and short-term mission (STM) trips we offer to students. Most youth ministries include some sort of service element in their ministry calendars. So we schedule a Saturday service blitz, an inner-city overnighter, or a week-long jaunt to the Dominican Republic all in the name of transformational ministry. Yet before we pass around our next clipboard and invite kids to sign up, we may want to ask a probing question: Are our service and mission events equivalent to the CNN news crawl—making us all think we're "world Christians" when, in reality, we're like tourists who are just passing through before we return to life as usual?

Plus, what about the impact on those we're supposedly serving? While we might feel better about ourselves because we've gotten dirty for Jesus, have we really made a difference? Recent research suggests our service trips and experiences might not produce the spiritual and relational bang we expect. At least not in the long term.

Consider these relatively new research findings:[2]

> The explosive growth in the number of STM trips among both teenagers and adults has not been accompanied by similarly explosive growth in the number of career missionaries.

> It's not clear whether participation in STM trips causes participants to give more money to alleviate poverty once life returns to normal.

> Participating in a STM trip does not seem to reduce participants' tendencies toward materialism.

To paraphrase the *Field of Dreams* mantra: If we send them, they will grow...kinda.

Not-So-Essential Service Versus Essential Justice

As you and I come to terms with the bad news that our service is more superficial than we had hoped, we're eager for new tools and paradigms to help us make an essential impact on our kids and our world. One such new paradigm benefiting many youth ministries is an understanding of the difference between service and social justice. Social justice goes a step further than service by trying not only to alleviate suffering but also to right the wrongs that created the suffering in the first place.

Service is a high calling and a vital part of following Jesus. But Jesus' call to love is also a call to look for more lasting solutions.

One way to describe this difference is that service is offering a thirsty person a cold glass of water. But social justice is asking why the thirsty person needs a cold glass of water in the first place and then doing what it takes so the thirsty person can get his own water in the future.

Learning from the Justice Experts

For the past three years, we at the Fuller Youth Institute (in collaboration with Dave Livermore of the Global Learning Center at Grand Rapids Theological Seminary and Terry Linhart of Bethel College, Indiana) have convened two summits of experts in youth short-term missions.[3] During those summits we've asked tough questions such as:

> How can our service work be part of God's justice?

> How do we move service beyond spiritual tourism?

> What vital theological threads should weave their way through our service?

> How can we move beyond rhetoric to true partnership with those we're serving?

As we've searched high and low for relevant research and tools, one theme has repeatedly emerged everywhere we've looked: We need to do a better job of walking with students before, during, and after their service.

Let's be honest. Our preparation before the service experience usually consists of M&Ms: Money and Medical Releases. Our reflection during the trip boils down to a few minutes of prayer requests before our team tumbles into bed, exhausted. And our debriefing after we get home is little more than organizing the media show and the testimonies to share in church.

If we want greater transformation, then we need a completely different time frame for our service. Perhaps instead of viewing an inner-city trip as just three days, we need to view it as a three-month process. Instead of looking at a week in the Dominican Republic as seven days, we need to think of it as a seven-month journey.

What Do We Do With All That Time?

What do we do with all those extra weeks before and after our service experience? And how do we squeeze every ounce of impact out of the time we're doing mission work?

We recommend an experiential education framework originally proposed by Laura Joplin[4] and later modified and tested by Terry Linhart[5] on youth STM trips.

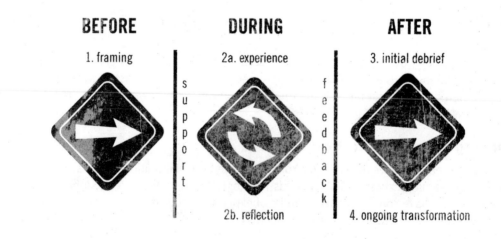

BEFORE	DURING	AFTER
1. framing	2a. experience	3. initial debrief
	2b. reflection	4. ongoing transformation

support — feedback

Step One (Before): Framing

A successful service or learning experience starts when we help students *frame* the sometimes mind-blowing and other times menial experiences that await them. More than just helping them raise money, learn a drama, or know what to pack, research indicates that our job as youth workers is to facilitate a series of gatherings and events to prepare students emotionally, mentally, spiritually, and relationally for their upcoming justice work. If we don't, we're cheating them out of the true value of what lies ahead.

Step Two (During): Experience—Reflection

The main component in students' learning during their actual service is the *experience-reflection* cycle. In this ongoing feedback loop, you and your students are placed in situations and activities that purposefully stretch you. Maybe you're using new skill muscles in a cross-cultural setting that's unfamiliar to you. Or maybe your group is tired, cranky, or hungry, and the glue that has united you up to this point is dissolving.

Whatever your students are experiencing, they're constantly assigning meaning to it. Although usually unconscious of it, teenagers are continually engaged in a highly personal, ongoing conversation in their own minds about who they are in relation to God, to others, and to their futures.

The constant barrage of experiences on a typical service adventure comes at students so fast and furiously, they often feel as if they're sprinting through a museum, barely viewing its masterpieces out of the corners of their eyes. As adult youth workers our job is to give students space to catch their breath and ask questions to help them decipher the deep meaning behind their observations, thoughts, and feelings.

Step Three (After): Initial Debrief

At the culmination of your experience, as your students' minds and your ministry's minivans start heading for home, you've now entered the third step of *initial debrief*. Maybe it's the last day of your STM trip as you take a bit of time for R and R, or perhaps it's when you hit a coffee shop together for 30 minutes after you've visited patients at the local children's hospital. Either way, the goal is to gather your team together after the "work" is completed to start the even harder work of long-term transformation.

Step Four (After): Ongoing Transformation

If most youth groups lack an effective preservice *framing* time, then even more of them have difficulty facilitating proper *ongoing transformation*. Two realities fight against effective learning transfer. First, most of the significant growth in a service experience takes place in an environment that's very different from the students' home communities. Second, the students don't know how to translate the learning to their own lives. That's why they need us to help them connect the dots between having lunch with a homeless man in Detroit and having lunch with a new kid in their school cafeteria one month later.

Through It All: Support and Feedback

To facilitate the *experience-reflection* cycle, Joplin recommends surrounding the discussions and activities with walls of support and feedback. While these two expressions of care are vital throughout the process, their importance peaks during the time you're actually serving.

Your default may be to assume that *support* and *feedback* best flow from the other adults and students on your team. While this is often true, the best networks stretch far beyond the immediate team. Research shows a strong correlation between individuals' success in a cross-cultural experience and the emotional and tangible support they receive from their friends and family. Plus, let's not forget the locals we're serving. Many of them can wrap your students in the type of love that both comforts and convicts.

How long does the process take?

By now you might be wondering if the before/during/after model is something you progress through only once during the many months involved in your justice work or if it's something you progress through *many times*. The answer is *both*. Part of the beauty of this model is that you can walk through it in a morning, in a week, or during a year-long emphasis on service or mission.

If you're planning a one-week trip to an inner city two hours away, then your time frame might look something like this:

BEFORE	DURING	AFTER
three months	one week	three months

If you're planning a three-hour visit to the local rescue mission, your time frame might look more like this:

BEFORE	DURING	AFTER
one hour	three hours	one hour

If you're planning a three-hour visit to the local rescue mission, your time frame might look more like this:

The news crawl is designed to keep us informed as quickly and conveniently as possible. Essential justice does just the opposite: It invites us to the longer and harder—but more rewarding—ride of seeing God right the wrongs around us.

ESSENTIAL TEAM TALK

The Big Idea: Improved reflection with students before, during, and after our service experiences can move us into more essential justice.

You'll need—

> Either ice cream or Starbucks coffee for your volunteers as an initial snack. If you're doing Starbucks, make sure to contact your volunteers ahead of time to get their orders. (Have a paper and pen handy for some of those long ones, like my personal favorite: A grande caffè vanilla Frappuccino, double blended, no whipped cream.)

> A whiteboard

> Markers

> Bibles

> Tape

> An *Essential Leadership Participant's Guide* for each of your adult volunteers

> Have More Time? option: Copies of the following Not-So-Essential Service Versus Essential Justice table

Now

Give out your ice cream or Starbucks treats and touch base on the action plan that your team developed during your previous team meetings. Celebrate what God and your team have done and pinpoint future next steps.

Transition to the topic of essential justice by inviting your leaders to turn to the Now section of their *Participant's Guide* and then asking—

> Q: **How much would you guess our country spends in a year on treats like the ones we had today?**

Field answers and then write the correct answer on the whiteboard. In the case of Starbucks, it's about $10 billion in revenue (most of which comes from sales in the United States).[6] Americans also spend an estimated $20 billion on ice cream per year.[7]

Continue: **Let's contrast that with some of the needs of our world.**

Write the following statistics on the whiteboard: **According to the United Nations, providing clean water and basic sanitation for the entire world would cost _$7 billion_ a year for the next 10 years. An additional _$4 billion a year_ for the next 10 years could finance basic health care that would prevent the deaths of 3 million infants each year.**[8]

Q: **As you compare those statistics with the amount of money we spend on treats like** (whatever treat you brought in), **what are your thoughts and feelings?**

Q: **If you had to give our ministry a grade for the way we right the wrongs around us (either locally or globally), what would it be? Explain your answer.**

Q: **What have been some of the best service experiences we've offered our students? What made them so effective?**

Q: **Some of the best research on short-term missions and service reveals that much of the transformation teenagers experience during such experiences is short-term at best. What in our ministry would confirm this finding? What would contradict it?**

New

Continue: **In 2006 MTV conducted a nationwide survey to understand how and why American teenagers are active in social causes.**[9] **Let's look at their findings and compare them with our own teenagers.**

Finding 1: Of the kids they surveyed, _70 percent_ say it's important to help others in need. Only _19 percent_ are "very involved" in doing so.

Q: **In what ways does this finding reflect the reality of our kids?**

Finding 2: The Top Five reasons kids aren't involved are—
> It's _just not for me_ (18 percent).
> I like to hang out with friends (15 percent).
> I don't have _enough time_ (14 percent).
> I don't know how to get started (14 percent).
> I want to see concrete results (8 percent).

Q: **Which of these reasons are true for our students? What other reasons might our kids give that aren't on this MTV list?**

Finding 3: _62 percent_ of teenagers say the issues that matter most to them are those that have touched them or someone they know.

Q: Which justice issues seem to touch our students the most?

Finding 4: 70 percent of teens involved in activism report that their _parents_' encouragement played a major role in their choice to get involved.

Q: What role do parents play in our students' interest in justice work?

Q: What role do we _wish_ parents played?

Finding 5: The Top Two factors that would motivate kids to be more involved are:

1. If they could do the activity _with their friends_.

2. If they had _more time_ to volunteer or more convenient volunteer activities.

Q: How do we see friendship impacting our students' choices to serve? How about service activities that are easily accessible to teenagers?

Continue: **As we think about our roles in creating space for the Holy Spirit to transform students into kingdom people, one new theme emerges from the MTV findings: Justice needs to hit our kids close to _home_. It needs to be in their homes literally—as we invite parents both to exemplify and to encourage their own kids to right the wrongs around them. It needs to hit close to home thematically—as we help students understand how particular injustices relate to their lives. It needs to hit home logistically—as we offer opportunities students can do at various times and at various levels of intensity. It needs to hit home personally—as we expose our students to people who have been oppressed, thereby giving injustice a face and a name. And justice ministry needs to hit home relationally—as we help teens right wrongs in partnership with their friends.**

How

Explain: **According to Fuller Youth Institute research, it's often youth workers' _conversations_ with their students that help hit home the plight of the "least of these."**

At this point walk through the steps in the Before/During/After model explained in Essential Thoughts (see following diagrams).

Have More Time?

Consider reviewing the following Not-So-Essential Service Versus Essential Justice table with your leaders. After you've finished invite your leaders to comment on which areas of your ministry reflect essential justice and which reflect not-so-essential service.

Not-So-Essential Service Versus Essential Justice

Not-So-Essential Service	Essential Justice
Service makes us feel like a great savior who rescues the broken.	Justice means God does the rescuing, but God often works through the united power of his great and diverse community to do it.
Service often dehumanizes (even if only subtly) those who are labeled the receivers.	Justice restores human dignity by creating an environment in which all involved give and receive in a spirit of reciprocal learning and mutual ministry.
Service is something we do for others.	Justice is something we do with others.
Service is an event.	Justice is a lifestyle.
Service expects results immediately.	Justice hopes for results sometime soon but recognizes that systemic change takes time.
The goal of service is to help others.	The goal of justice is to remove obstacles so others can help themselves.
Service focuses on what our own ministry can accomplish.	Justice focuses on how we can work with other ministries to accomplish even more.

BEFORE/DURING/AFTER MODEL

One-Week Trip to an Inner City

BEFORE	DURING	AFTER
three months	one week	three months

Three-Hour Visit to the Local Rescue Mission

BEFORE	DURING	AFTER
one hour	three hours	one hour

Now ask these questions:

Q: **Which of these steps do we do well? Why do you say that?**

Q: **Which of these steps represent growth areas for us? Why?**

As a team discuss an upcoming service experience you're planning for your students and view it through the grid of the Before/During/After model. Then ask—

Q: **What could we do to more powerfully frame the experience for our students?**

Q: **How can we help them reflect more effectively in the midst of their justice work?**

Q: **What ideas would help our initial debrief?**

Q: **What could we do that would more likely lead to ongoing transformation?**

Q: **As adult leaders what tangible actions can we take to provide essential support and feedback? How can we also involve students' families in giving support? What about other adults from our church?**

Invite your leaders to turn to the Essential Justice Action Plan at the end of the chapter in their *Participant's Guide* and use its rows as a way to pinpoint specific goals, action steps, and prayer requests, especially in light of any upcoming justice work in your ministry.

To wrap up your discussion, invite your leaders to turn to Amos 5:21-24 (it's provided in their *Participant's Guide*) and ask for a volunteer to read the passage:

Essential Justice Action Plan

Our team's ideas for how to move forward into essential justice include:

OVERALL GOALS	ACTION STEPS TOWARD THESE GOALS	SPECIFIC PRAYER REQUESTS	SIGNS OF GOD'S ACTIVITY

I hate, I despise your religious festivals; I cannot stand your assemblies. Even though you bring me burnt offerings and grain offerings, I will not accept them. Though you bring choice fellowship offerings, I will have no regard for them. Away with the noise of your songs! I will not listen to the music of your harps. But let justice roll on like a river, righteousness like a never-failing stream! (Amos 5:21-24)

Ask, **Why do you think God doesn't accept the people's offerings and religious acts?**

Close in prayer by giving your leaders time to confess out loud the ways they—either individually or corporately—have neglected kingdom justice. After a time of public confession, read Amos 5:24 again and invite your leaders to pray out loud for God's justice to roll like a river through your ministry, city, and world. Ask God to keep every leader and every parent sensitive to how they can cooperate with the justice work that God longs to do through your students and your ministry.

ENDNOTES: CHAPTER FOUR

Essential Justice: Moving Beyond the News Crawl

1. This section is adapted from an article entitled "If We Send Them, They Will Grow… Maybe" by Kara Powell, Brad Griffin, Terry Linhart, and Dave Livermore, available at www.fulleryouthinstitute.org, as well as from chapters 2 and 6 of *Deep Justice in a Broken World* (Grand Rapids, Mich.: Zondervan/Youth Specialties, 2008). The article was originally published in the March/April 2007 issue of *The Journal of Student Ministries*, © DevelopMinistries, www.developministries.com. Used with permission.

2. Robert J. Priest, Terry Dischinger, Steve Rasmussen, and C.M. Brown, "Researching the Short-Term Mission Movement," *Missiology* 34, no. 4 (October 2006), 431-450.

3. We are deeply indebted to our coresearchers Dave Livermore and Terry Linhart for the design and facilitation of these summits, in addition to all of the participants who sacrificially gave their time and deep insights: Jared Ayers, George Bache, Noel Becchetti, Terry Bley, Todd Bratulich, Tom Carpenter, Sean Cooper, April Diaz, Brian Dietz, Joel Fay, Brad Griffin, Hal Hamilton, Brian Heerwagen, Eric Iverson, Tom Ives, Cari Jenkins, Johnny Johnston, Kent Koteskey, Sandy Liu, Mark Maines, Mark Matlock, Daryl Nuss, Derry Prenkert, Kurt Rietema, David Russell, David Schultz, Rich Van Pelt, Bob Whittet, and Kimberly Williams.

4. Laura Joplin, "On Defining Experiential Education" in *The Theory of Experiential Education*, ed. K. Warren, M. Sakofs, and J. S. Hunt Jr. (Dubuque, Ia.: Kendall/Hunt Publishing, 1995), 15-22.

5. Terrence D. Linhart, "Planting Seeds: The Curricular Hope of Short Term Mission Experiences in Youth Ministry," *Christian Education Journal* series 3 (2005), 256-272. For the purposes of this curriculum, some of the terminology in the model has been modified.

6. Steve Kichen, "Revenue on Sale," *Stock Focus*, Forbes.com (Feb. 4, 2009), http://www.forbes.com/2009/02/04/starbucks-revenues-sales-personal-finance_0204_stock_scorecard.html.

7. Martha Wilson, "What Americans and Europeans Spend on Ice Cream: $31 Billion Global Cost of Creating Marine Parks to Protect the Oceans: $12-14 Billion," Press Release for the World Wildlife Fund (June 14, 2004), http://www.worldwildlife.org/who/media/press/2004/WWFPresitem726.html.

8. United Nations Development Programme, "Chapter 3: Aid for the 21st Century," Human Development Report 2005: International Cooperation at a Crossroads: Aid, Trade and Security in an Unequal World, 93–94, http://hdr.undp.org/en/reports/global/hdr2005/chapters/

9. MTV's national survey was composed of 1,187 12-to-24-year-olds who completed online surveys and 98 students who were interviewed personally. This research can be accessed for free at http://www.mtv.com/thinkmtv/research/ (click on "For a copy of the full Just Cause study and an appendix, click here to view the PDF").

CHAPTER FIVE

ESSENTIAL
FAMILY MINISTRY
PARTNERING WITH PARENTS

ESSENTIAL THOUGHTS[1]

You're getting ready to leave your weekly youth group gathering when out of the corner of your eye, you notice the mom of one of your students heading your way. Do you assume she's on her way over to...

A. Thank you for your influence on her daughter's life?

B. Point out that you're favoring another drummer in your worship team over her son?

C. Ask how she can pray for you?

D. Complain about how you locked her son in the trunk of your car as a practical joke?

E. You don't even take the time to guess; you head toward a side exit as quickly as you can.

As moms and dads have headed my way, I've made all of those assumptions. In fact, I've actually been in every single one of those scenarios multiple times. (Yes, I'm ashamed to admit that as a youth ministry rookie, I locked a ninth grade boy in the trunk of my car. But it only happened once; I learned my lesson the first time on that one!)

What is it that causes parents to seek us out? Especially if you're a parent yourself, you'll quickly get it: Parents love their kids and want the best for them.

You may think *you* love the kids in your ministry, but trust me, your love is dwarfed by their parents' love for them.

You might be wondering—*but what about the parents who don't seem to care that much about their kids? What about the moms and dads who drop off their kids at our youth ministry (if they make the effort to drop them off at all) and never come in and introduce themselves? What about the moms, stepmoms, dads, and stepdads who are emotionally unavailable to their kids, clueless about what their kids are really up to, or maybe even manifest behavior that is borderline (or across the line) neglectful or abusive?*

I'm not saying parents always make good decisions, are void of sin, or even know how to express their love properly. All I'm saying is that parents, at least at some level (usually a very deep level), love their kids.

When youth workers recognize this love and the greater impact they can have when parents and leaders work together to influence teenagers, they begin to talk about the importance of family ministry. However, even when they're convinced of its importance, many youth workers still don't know exactly how to do it.

But the good news is that you're probably doing more to positively impact families than you may realize. And the even better news is that as your team strategically evaluates the needs of your students and their families, you can stop running away from parents and their concerns and start running toward them.

The Three Modes of Family Ministry

Much of the family ministry you're doing right now or might envision doing in the future falls into one of three basic categories described by Dr. Chap Clark at Fuller Seminary:[2] (1) The Counseling/Care Mode, (2) The Nuclear Family Mode, and (3) The Church as Family Mode.

1. The Counseling/Care Mode: Guardrails and Emergency Rooms

WHAT IS IT? The counseling/care approach to family ministry manifests itself primarily through education and programs, many of which can be provided by professional counselors.

The first of two metaphors that help us understand the essence of the counseling/care mode is a guardrail. Guardrail programs are designed to help a family before a crisis even happens. Every family will face challenges, but advance training can help family members respond to those difficult stretches in a healthier manner. Youth workers can provide some of these guardrails by training families (especially parents and stepparents) in conflict resolution, youth culture, parent-youth communication, and adolescent development.

The second metaphor used in the counseling/care mode is an emergency room. In the church as emergency room model, your youth ministry is a place of healing and recovery where parents and kids can go once damage has been done. Some examples are programs that help students deal with their parents' divorce or that help family members navigate a teenager's drug or alcohol addiction. These programs guide families to lean on the surrounding community and, more importantly, on the God who ultimately brings healing and freedom.

STRENGTHS: The counseling/care mode acknowledges that real life is full of pain and hardship. Youth ministries are wise to offer practical training and support groups that meet the real needs of teenagers and their parents.

POTENTIAL PROBLEMS: Programs are the heart of this model, but often they aren't well attended. In addition, these programs are often disconnected from the rest of the church body. Participants become "the hurt people over there," while "we healthy people are the *real* church." There may not be a sense that the church is the place for hurting people—it only has programs for them.

2. The Nuclear Family Mode

WHAT IS IT? In the nuclear family mode of family ministry, parents are the primary spiritual nurturers of their children, and it's the church's job to equip parents to accomplish this task. Theologically, the nuclear family mode is rooted in an understanding that God designed the family as a unique hub of love and discipleship in the social order.

This mode is also rooted in the reality that children spend far more time with their families than they ever will at your ministry gatherings. While a student may be involved with your ministry for 40 to 200 hours a year, the same kid will potentially spend more than 3,000 hours a year with his family.

In this mode the church thereby serves the nuclear family by providing shared family experiences for parents and children together (think of events such as all-family game night or a father-daughter camp). The church also offers resources to help parents disciple their children. At its best the nuclear family model "aims at developing stronger family relationships so that families will be more effective witnesses and messengers of the love of Christ."[3]

STRENGTHS: Scripture affirms the unique quality of the parent-child relationship as well as the marriage relationship. Both the Old and New Testaments give specific attention to particular nuclear family relationships (see Deuteronomy 4:9-10, 6:6-8; and Ephesians 6:4).

POTENTIAL PROBLEMS: Parents often feel inadequate to be their kids' primary disciplers. In reality some parents occasionally are inadequate. Not all parents have the knowledge, ability, or resources to be their child's primary discipler. Also, this mode can potentially ignore the relationships and needs of nontraditional families and singles within a church. Only families that fit the typical "nuclear triad" of mother, father, and children can find the supportive environment they need.

Also, while this mode advocates and protects the family, it can also be internally focused in a harmful—even idolatrous—way. Families need to be supported and equipped to do God's work in the world, not simply to be happy families. If there is too much focus on finding happiness, then doing God's work may not happen.

Finally, a Western understanding of family may cause us to misunderstand the original intent of certain "family" passages in Scripture.[4] A family in the Old Testament would have included parents, children, workers, and perhaps adult siblings with their own spouses and children.

In fact, households could have been composed of as many as 80 people. Scriptural texts about child-rearing, such as the encouragement to impress God's commands on your children in Deuteronomy 6:6-8, likely refer to the communal raising of children. Our current cultural distance from these passages may cause us to put undue pressure on parents alone.

3. The Church as Family Mode

WHAT IS IT? The church as family mode understands that any person who claims to follow Christ is first and foremost a Christian before she's a family member. The church, then, has priority over nuclear family boundaries. As Rodney Clapp writes in *Families at the Crossroads*—

> Jesus creates a new family. It is the new first family, a family of his followers that now demands primary allegiance. In fact, it demands allegiance even over the old first family, the biological family. Those who do the will of the Father...are now brothers and sisters of Jesus and one another.[5]

Therefore, anyone in your church can form and maintain family ties with anyone else under the lordship of Jesus Christ.

STRENGTHS: The church as family mode is attentive to Jesus' teachings about a new kingdom family formed from those who do God's will (Mark 3:31-35). When done well, it also has the potential to emphasize the overall kingdom family while simultaneously supporting a student's biological family.

POTENTIAL PROBLEMS: If a church puts so much emphasis on community, inclusion, and taking care of everybody's needs, it could undermine the family system by not supporting its uniqueness. Churches who rely only on this mode may also struggle to tangibly support healthy family systems. For example, these mentalities may arise: *We don't preach healthy marriages because it will exclude the single mom, and we want to love her and be a family with her* or *We don't host a father-daughter banquet because it excludes all girls with nonexistent or toxic relationships with their fathers.* The key to operating in the church as family mode is to not undermine the family system even as your church creates a new family in Christ.

Essential Family Ministry Comes in Threes

Effective family ministry can take on a variety of expressions and forms based on the particular needs and resources of individual ministries. Yet it's critical to engage all three modes of ministry, layering them together to meet the variety of needs of your students and their families. As evident from their respective strengths and weaknesses, no one mode is adequate alone; the weaknesses of each are compensated by the opportunities of the others.

Do you find that you never offer any formal resources to families? Consider whom you might invite to offer practical training to the parents of your students. Is it time to get creative about an event geared for families? Then maybe offer a family justice service project or a day hike.

Or could your students benefit from the introduction of some new faces—such as the seniors or the young children in your community—as a more full experience of God's kingdom?

One final note as you brainstorm: The goal isn't to add more programs to your already full calendar. You don't need that; your students don't need that; and the mom headed your way after youth group certainly doesn't need that either. What we do need are spaces and places for us to link arms with possibly the only people on the planet who care even more about the kids in our group than we do: Their families.

ESSENTIAL TEAM TALK

The Big Idea: By understanding the unique needs and experiences of the families in your ministry, you can creatively and strategically meet those needs and further your students' faith.

You'll need—

> A Parent Panel: Ahead of time, contact a handful of thoughtful and authentic parents of your students and invite them to participate in your panel. Give them copies of the fill-in-the-blank statements mentioned in the Now section so they can prepare in advance.

> Three sheets of poster paper (We recommend using poster paper instead of a whiteboard, as you'll want to keep what you've written.)

> Pens

> Tape

> An *Essential Leadership Participant's Guide* for each of your adult volunteers

Now

Greet your volunteers as well as the parents joining you for the Parent Panel. Before you dive into the panel, touch base on the action plan that your team developed during your previous team meetings. Celebrate what God and your team have done, and pinpoint future next steps.

Transition to the Parent Panel by explaining the goal: To help the youth ministry team understand the needs, dreams, and perspectives of parents. Ask the members of your panel to introduce themselves and share the names and ages of their children. One at a time, read each of the following fill-in-the-blank statements and invite the panelists to respond. As they do, encourage your volunteers, or the other parent panelists, to ask follow-up questions or make follow-up comments.

> I feel affirmed as a parent when…

> I feel insecure as a parent when…

> As a parent, I love that this youth ministry…

> As a parent, I wish this youth ministry…

> The best thing you're currently doing to support my relationship with my kid is…

> The best thing you could do to support my relationship with my kid is…

> I love it when you help my kid understand…

> I wish you would help my kid understand…

> Please don't stop…

> Please stop…

> I would love to receive training that would help me…

> You might not realize this, but…

After the Parent Panel is finished, thank your students' parents for participating and ask a few of your volunteers to pray for them and ask for wisdom in how to better serve and love kids' families. Excuse your students' parents and ask your volunteers to turn to the Essential Team Talk section of their *Participant's Guide*. Then discuss these questions:

Q: **What themes did you notice in the comments of the members of the Parent Panel?** It's quite possible that the parents' comments might provoke some deep emotions in your staff, so make sure you give space and time for your volunteers honestly to share their reflections.

Q: **What in this panel confirmed what you might have suspected?**

Q: **What, if anything, surprised you?**

New

Spend some time reviewing the three modes of family ministry presented in the Essential Thoughts article at the beginning of this chapter in this book and in the *Participant's Guide*. Make sure your volunteers understand the essence of each mode and its respective strengths and weaknesses.

Use tape to post three pieces of poster paper along the front wall of your meeting space. Write COUNSELING/CARE MODE on the left sheet of poster paper, NUCLEAR FAMILY MODE on the middle sheet, and CHURCH AS FAMILY MODE on the last sheet.

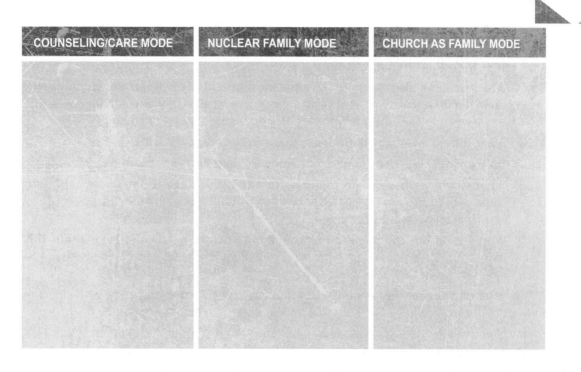

COUNSELING/CARE MODE	NUCLEAR FAMILY MODE	CHURCH AS FAMILY MODE

Ask—

Q: **What is our youth ministry already doing that reflects these three modes?** Write your volunteers' answers on the appropriate sheets of poster paper. If fitting, feel free to ask these additional questions:

Q: **What is our church as a whole already doing that reflects these three modes?**

Q: **What have we learned about the way our youth ministry serves students' families?**

Q: **Do we tend to favor one or two of these three modes? Which ones? How do you feel about that?**

Underline what you're currently doing on each sheet of poster paper. Then say, **Now let's do a bit of dreaming.**

Q: **Based on what we heard from our Parent Panel or what you know about our kids and their parents, what new ideas do you have to help us be more effective in these three modes? These might be brand-new ideas, or they might be tweaks on what we already do. Let's do some creative brainstorming...**

Write your team members' ideas on the appropriate sheets of poster paper and feel free to add additional sheets if you run out of room (which would be a good problem to have!).

How

After you're finished brainstorming, ask:

Q: **Which of these ideas seem to have the most potential to impact our students and their families?** Based on your team's input, begin to identify a handful of ideas that would seem to have the most leverage in your family ministry efforts.

Q: **What difference might these ideas make in our students' lives?**

Q: **How might these ideas impact our students' families?**

Q: **What would we have to do to move from the idea stage to the implementation stage with these ideas?** Feel free to focus your implementation brainstorming on a few ideas that seem the most significant.

Q: **Who else in our congregation or community do we need to engage about this issue?** This could be the family ministry committee or department (if one exists), children's ministries, and senior leadership.

The idea is to begin to see natural connections between what may already be happening and to look for ways to integrate those things with your youth ministry strategies.

Invite your leaders to turn to the Essential Family Ministry Action Plan in their *Participant's Guide* and use its rows as a way to pinpoint specific goals, action steps, and prayer requests

Close in prayer using one-sentence prayers for the parents of the students in your ministry. After each one-sentence prayer, the rest of your team should agree by saying together, "May your grace be abundant in our families, oh Lord."

Point out that this phrase appears in the *Participant's Guide* so your volunteers can be more focused on prayer than on trying to remember the sentence. Begin by praying for any parents who are in the room and then pray for your students' parents more broadly.

Essential Family Ministry Action Plan

Our team's ideas for how to move forward into essential family ministry include:

OVERALL GOALS	ACTION STEPS TOWARD THESE GOALS	SPECIFIC PRAYER REQUESTS	SIGNS OF GOD'S ACTIVITY

Have More Time?

Odds are good that some of your volunteers aren't parents, some are parents of young children, some are parents of teens, and others are parents of former teenagers (meaning their children are now adults). Divide up your team into the appropriate life stage small groups. If your team of volunteers is on the smaller side and it doesn't make sense to divide up into smaller groups, then feel free to discuss these questions together in a large group since the answers will help your leaders understand each other.

Q: What opportunities are there for you to minister to students' families given your life stage?

Q: What challenges exist in family ministry because of your life stage?

Q: What specific steps would you like to take during the next few months with the families of the students you're closest to?

ENDNOTES: CHAPTER FIVE

Essential Family Ministry: Partnering With Parents

1. This section is adapted from an article by Meredith Miller entitled "Family Ministry: Good Things Come in Threes" (September 5, 2007), available at www.fulleryouthinstitute.org.

2. Dr. Chap Clark, Family Ministry Lectures at Fuller Theological Seminary. See also Chap Clark, *The Youth Worker's Handbook to Family Ministry: Strategies and Practical Ideas for Reaching Your Students' Families* (Grand Rapids, Mich.: Zondervan, 1997).

3. Diana R. Garland, *Family Ministry: A Comprehensive Guide* (Downers Grove, Ill.: InterVarsity Press, 1999), 377.

4. Ray S. Anderson and Dennis B. Guernsey, *On Being Family: A Social Theology of the Family* (Grand Rapids, Mich.: Eerdmans Publishing, 1985), 31.

5. Rodney Clapp, *Families at the Crossroads: Beyond Traditional and Modern Options* (Downers Grove, Ill.: InterVarsity Press, 1993), 77.

CHAPTER SIX

ESSENTIAL INTERGENERATIONAL MINISTRY
FROM "BIG CHURCH" TO "OUR CHURCH"

ESSENTIAL THOUGHTS[1]

"Big church."

In my early days as a youth worker, that was the label I slapped on my church's events and worship services outside of our youth ministry. They were all big church, and we were the youth ministry (or whatever catchy name du jour we were calling ourselves and our Sunday and mid-week gatherings).

The rest of the church had the senior pastor; the youth ministry had... well...my colleagues and me. The rest of the church had their buildings, and we had the youth room. The rest of the church had their worship services, and we had our Sunday meeting, which felt a lot like a self-contained youth worship service. Sure, we encouraged our students to go to the church service that met after our Sunday morning service, but most families skipped out as soon as the youth service ended.

Twice a year on Youth Sunday, our youth ministry took over the big church Sunday evening worship services. Our students were ushers; our youth band led worship; and one of our youth leaders preached. We planned and prayed as if our involvement was going to transform our church. In reality, it felt more like we were performing in front of a congregation of adults who seemed to have one of two responses: Either *Isn't that cute?* or *I can tolerate this for one week as long as the* real *minister and music leaders are back next Sunday.*

A Secret Segregation

More and more churches and leaders are shining a spotlight on the racial segregation that has tragically made 11 a.m. on Sundays one of the most racially segregated hours in America.[2] But few of us are shining the same spotlight on a second form of segregation that also divides us as believers—age segregation.

Please don't misunderstand me: I'm all for dedicated (and even paid) youth workers who can give specialized attention to the developmental and faith challenges of teenagers. Sixteen-year-olds need a space and place to have honest and authentic conversations with their peers about life, Jesus, and the relevance of one to the other. As one youth leader told us, "No one wants to talk about masturbation with Grandma in the room."

However, one of my life mantras is this: Balance is something we swing through on our way to the other extreme. As churches have appropriately tried to give teenagers their own spaces and places, we've swung the pendulum too far in the other direction and created youth ministry enclaves separate from the "big church."

So what does it look like not only to tolerate, but also to welcome teenagers into the full life of the church? How can we create communities of faith in which the gifts and passions of all—regardless of age—show the power of the full church to be changed by Jesus in order to change the world? Perhaps we should start by exploring how the ultimate Youth Worker (yup, we mean Jesus) wants us to eliminate the distance between the youth ministry and the "big church" and instead unite both in God's kingdom vision of "our church."

Involving Kids in Church à la Jesus

As a mother of preschoolers, I've spent a lot of time perusing children's Bibles. Most of them have a picture on the cover of a smiling Jesus who's typically sitting and surrounded by seven or eight smiling boys and girls. As youth workers we tend to look at those pictures of a smiling Jesus surrounded by smiling children and have the same sort of reaction my church had toward Youth Sunday: "Isn't that cute?"

In reality, Jesus' interactions with children were far from cute; they were both radical and revolutionary.

The Old Testament view of kids

To better understand the context of Jesus' interactions with children, we first need to examine the view of children in the Old Testament. According to Dr. Judith Gundry-Volf of Yale University, children in the Old Testament Jewish tradition were viewed as a divine gift and sign of God's blessing. An abundance of children was equated with an abundance of blessing and joy (Psalm

127:3-5, Psalm 128:3-6). Childlessness was wretched, and Old Testament Jews took drastic and unusual measures to overcome it (Genesis 30:1-22, Deuteronomy 25:5-10, and 1 Samuel 1).[3]

The first-century view of kids

At the time of the writing of the Gospels, in many ways the cultural pendulum had swung toward a more negative view of children. In the Greco-Roman world children weren't viewed as equal persons. Instead, they were among the least-valued members of society. Harsh discipline, abandonment, and infanticide were allowable practices if they were the wishes of the child's father.[4]

According to Dionysius of Halicarnassus, "The law-giver of the Romans gave virtually full power to the father over his son, whether he thought proper to imprison him, to scourge him, to put him in chains, and keep him at work in the fields, or to put him to death."[5] Probably more common than this type of extreme treatment of children as some sort of property was simply the view that childhood was a training ground for adult life, not a significant stage of life in itself.[6]

Jesus' entry as an infant

In the midst of these mixed and often negative messages about the value of children, Jesus, the Messiah, entered the world as a newborn. Perhaps 20 centuries later, the radical nature of Jesus' entry as a baby has been somewhat obscured. Yet the provocative nature of this entry is a powerful image for those of us in youth ministry. The fifth-century patriarch of Constantinople, Nestorius, was so struck by the implications of this that he wrote, "I deny that God is two or three months old."[7] The 20th-century theologian Karl Barth wrote in astonishment of the baby Jesus, "This is your God!"[8]

Jesus' link between greatness and children

The radical nature of Jesus' birth is echoed in his radical link between childhood and greatness. In Luke 9:46 an argument broke out among Jesus' disciples about who was the greatest. The timing of this dispute makes sense in the overall context of Luke 9:28-45. In verses 28 to 36, Jesus took three disciples (Peter, James, and John, often referred to as the three who were closest to Jesus) to a mountain to pray. Perhaps the selection of those three and the exclusion of the others fueled feelings of jealousy and insecurity in the nine left behind. And the fact that those who were left behind were unable to heal a demon-possessed boy likely made them feel even more inferior and resentful (Luke 9:37-43).

Knowing about the disciples' argument over greatness, Jesus had a little child stand beside him. Then he taught, using these famous words: "Whoever welcomes this little child in my name welcomes me; and whoever welcomes me welcomes the one who sent me. For he who is the least among you all—he is the greatest" (Luke 9:48, NIV).

Thus Jesus placed two figures before the disciples: Himself, whom they greatly respected, and a child, who probably held little intrinsic value in their eyes. Yet Jesus showed the inestimable but hidden value of children by linking them to greatness. The good news for the disciples was that greatness can be pursued and possessed. The bad news for the disciples was that greatness didn't come in a manner familiar to them. It didn't come from comparison with others, as they had assumed. It came by welcoming a child, who in being the least somehow became the greatest. As Jesus often did, he showed that the kingdom of God is an upside-down kingdom with upside-down values.

An understanding of the Greek language that Jesus used in this well-known statement about embracing kids makes his words all the more revolutionary. The Greek verb Jesus used here for "welcome" is *dechomai* (pronounced "DECK-oh-my"), which was often used in the context of showing hospitality to guests. Thus it carries a certain connotation of servanthood. What makes Jesus' teaching all the more remarkable is that in the first century, taking care of children was a task generally fulfilled by members of the culture who were viewed as different and even inferior to the male disciples—meaning women and slaves.[9]

Thus Jesus was asking the disciples who had just been arguing about their individual greatness to show utmost humility and esteem by embracing the kids in their midst.

Fast-Forward 2,000 Years

So in the midst of the current church trend of separating 16-year-olds from 56-year-olds, what radical (and at times not-so-radical) steps can your youth ministry take to follow Jesus' example and teaching regarding welcoming and valuing kids in your community of faith?

Experiment with intergenerational worship

Many smaller churches do a great job of weaving students into the life of their corporate worship. But once churches get big enough to have a youth ministry budget, teenagers often no longer sing in the choir or read the Bible in "big church." Whatever your church's worship style or approach, students can be meaningfully involved in a number of creative ways.

One church shared with us that they started reincorporating students into worship by setting aside an entire church season (for example, Lent or Advent) to worship together as a whole church. They divided the church into groups who studied, brainstormed, and planned creative aspects of each week's worship service and opened wide the doors for youth participation. They found that while the process wasn't perfect and some students—and adults—were certainly resistant, overall the church grew tremendously in its appreciation for the contributions from people of every age in corporate worship.

Mentors and small group leaders

So often we as youth workers try to recruit the youngest possible adult volunteers as small group leaders and mentors. While a college student has a lot to bring to youth ministry, youth workers too often overlook the valuable life experience that older adults can pour into the lives of teenagers. (Most of the contributors to this book started in youth ministry while we were still in college, so we're not against it!)

One of our best junior high girls' small group leaders was Jean, a lady in her 70s who had nothing cool or hip to offer those girls. But she was willing to sit and listen to them week after week, sharing the drama of middle school life and offering wisdom and prayer for these surrogate granddaughters. Although not every 70-year-old is as sensitive or as willing as Jean, there are a lot more Jeans out there than you and your team may have assumed.

Service and justice work

From caring for local shut-ins to traveling across the world on a mission trip, service and care given in the name of Jesus need not be an age-exclusive enterprise. When we begin to see the entire church as the family of God, we see new service opportunities for students and adults of every age. At your next youth ministry justice experience, encourage students to invite their parents and grandparents or consider inviting one or two adult classes from your church to join you. Not only is this good for your students and your church, but it's also good for the locals with whom you'll be interacting to see your entire church family in action together.

Skill development

Some churches connect generations by setting up skill-transferring relationships between older and younger members. This might be as simple and brief as an afternoon small group session on basic car maintenance, or as involved as a year-long apprenticeship learning an adult's trade or professional skills. While some wonder how this contributes to teenagers' spiritual development, we argue that students need a whole-life approach to their faith, and the best way to learn it is to watch someone live it out in all aspects of life.

These days when I say "big church," I'm no longer talking about what the adults do while children and teenagers do something different. Instead, I'm hoping to move our congregation toward seeing that big church is who we are as a church family every day, all year long.

ESSENTIAL TEAM TALK

The Big Idea: In big and little ways, we can change our ministry and church programs to create more meaningful adult-student interaction.

You'll need—

> Two types of circular cookies, making sure one type is bigger than the other

> Poster paper (We recommend using poster paper instead of a whiteboard, as you'll want to keep your drawings.)

> Markers

> Tape

> Optional: Copies of your youth ministry calendar

> Optional: Copies of your overall church calendar. If that's difficult to get, then a list of major church events for the next six months will suffice.

> An *Essential Leadership Participant's Guide* for each of your adult volunteers

Now

Greet your adult volunteers and check to see how they're doing. Before you dive into a discussion about essential intergenerational ministry, touch base on the action plan your team developed during your previous team meetings. Celebrate what God and your team have done and pinpoint future next steps.

Next, distribute the cookies and ask each adult to take one or more of each type of cookie (depending on how much of your budget you spent on cookies).

Hold up the bigger cookie and explain: **Imagine this big cookie is a church. If I were to use these two cookies to describe the relationship most church youth ministries in the United States have with their own church, here's what I would do.**

At this point put the smaller cookie at the top of the big cookie, as if the two together were a one-eared Mickey Mouse.

ONE-EARED MICKEY MOUSE

Ask: **When these two cookies are positioned like this, what do they look like?** Field some answers from your team members. (And yes, they can eat their cookies as you continue with the discussion.)

Invite your team to turn to the Now section in their *Participant's Guide* and continue: **These two cookies remind me of a one-eared Mickey Mouse.**

Q: **In 1989 a youth worker wrote an article describing the relationship between the church and the typical youth ministry as a one-eared Mickey Mouse.**[10] **In what ways is that true of a typical church and youth ministry?**

Q: **In what ways is that true of our youth ministry?**

Q: **In what ways is that *not* true of our youth ministry?**

Q: **Imagine that you're supposed to defend the separation that currently exists between teens and adults in our church. What would you say?**

Q: **Now imagine you want to make the case for integrating our teenagers more into the life of the overall church. What would your main points be?**

Q: **What messages are sent to teenagers when they have very little overlap with the adults in the church?**

Q: **What messages are sent to the adults in the church when they don't regularly interact with teenagers?**

Continue: **As I mentioned previously, the term "one-eared Mickey Mouse" was coined in 1989. Based on what you know about youth culture and youth ministry, would you guess the separation between the overall church and teenagers has increased or decreased since then?**

New

Q: **If the one-eared Mickey Mouse isn't our ideal, then how would you describe the ideal level of intersection we'd want between the adults and the teenagers in our church? Is it total overlap, total separation, or somewhere in between? If it's somewhere in between, then would you lean more toward separation or overlap? Why?**

Give your leaders time to draw or describe their ideas in their *Participant's Guide* and then share them with the group.

Then say: **Based on what we've just shared with each other, do we have some sort of consensus about the type of engagement we'd like between our students and our church? If so, what is it?**

Dr. Chap Clark from Fuller Seminary gives us a tangible goal for increased adult-kid interaction. Chap suggests that we reverse the typical adult-student ratio in our youth ministry. Often in our youth ministry we talk about wanting to have one adult for every five (or insert whatever number is common in your setting) **students. So we'll periodically talk about having one adult for every five kids on our retreat or one adult for every five kids when we divide into small groups.**

What if we reverse that ratio? What if we had five adults pouring into each student? No, that doesn't mean five Bible study leaders but five adults who are somehow investing in a teenager. What would that do to our students?

After some discussion, ask:

Q: **What impact would a different adult-student ratio have on the adults in our church?**

Q: **What are some ways we could come closer to a five-to-one ratio?**

At this point you might want to highlight some of the ideas included in the Essential Thoughts article, especially those about intergenerational worship, service, mentoring, and skill development.

How

Continue: **All of those are great ideas, and I'd love for us to think about simple and even small changes we could make that might produce big results.**

Use tape to post your poster paper on the front wall of your meeting space. Then draw a picture of the path the typical teenager takes from the moment he or she pulls up to the parking lot for a typical church gathering (Sunday morning, for example) until the time the gathering ends and he or she drives out of that same parking lot. Make sure to include teenage hot spots, such as the bathrooms, available food (especially free food), and any other places where teens tend to congregate. You might practice this drawing ahead of time to make sure you don't omit any important teenage hangout.

Get your team members' input on the typical teenage path and then ask: **At what points in this path does the typical student in our ministry interact with adults?**

Mark each of those places on your map with an X.

Now write on your poster paper FIVE ADULTS TO ONE KID. Grab a different colored marker and ask: **Now if we want to move toward a new five-to-one ratio, what are some of the additional points along this path that we could use as catalysts for greater adult-kid interaction?**

Get your volunteers' ideas and mark them with stars. Encourage your team to think of very simple points of interaction, such as encouraging adults to ask (and then try to remember!) a teenager's name or inviting adults to ask a teenager how they can be praying for him. Follow up the next week to see how God is working in that area.

Now ask:

Q: **What have you learned about the typical teenager in our ministry as a result of our mapping exercise?**

Q: **What have you learned about our church?**

Q: **Which of the stars on this map are the most doable?**

Q: **Which of the stars on this map might have the greatest effect on our teenagers?**

Q: **Given their feasibility and impact, which stars do you think we should try to work on?**

Q: **What can we do to try to make those starred locations hot spots of student-adult interaction?**

Q: **How could we remap the student path—or the adult path—through our church to promote more cross-generational interactions?**

Q: **We'll be far more effective in making changes if we have the support of key church leaders. Who should we talk to about moving toward our five-to-one goal?**

Have More Time?

Distribute your church's calendar of events and ask: Which of these represents potential for quality student-adult interaction? In what ways might two of these events be modified to make them more appealing and more welcoming for our students?

Similarly, you could distribute your youth ministry's calendar and ask: Which of these events will likely have strong adult-kid interaction? Which two events have the greatest potential for such interaction? What changes need to be made to these events to facilitate such interaction?

Or you can divide your team in half and have one group discuss your church's calendar and the other your youth ministry's calendar. When those discussions are done, regroup and have each group share their thoughts.

Essential Intergenerational Ministry Action Plan

Our team's ideas for how to move forward into essential intergenerational ministry include:

OVERALL GOALS	ACTION STEPS TOWARD THESE GOALS	SPECIFIC PRAYER REQUESTS	SIGNS OF GOD'S ACTIVITY

Invite your leaders to turn to the Essential Intergenerational Ministry Action Plan (at the end of this chapter in their *Participant's Guide*) and use its rows as a way to pinpoint specific goals, action steps, and prayer requests.

If you're meeting at or near the location depicted on your map, close your training with a prayer walk. Follow the footsteps of a typical student in your ministry and pray for increased adult-student interaction along the way. If you're not meeting at or near that location, then close in prayer by gathering around the map you've drawn. Invite your volunteers to pray that students would sense the deep love and concern of the adults in your community at those specific locations, especially those marked by an X.

Keep the map and review it later as a team. If you have the opportunity, present the map to other ministers and leadership groups at your church as a powerful visual of the current state of adult-kid interaction, as well as the potential for essential intergenerational relationships.

ENDNOTES: CHAPTER SIX

Essential Intergenerational Ministry: From "Big Church" to "Our Church"

1. This section is adapted from an article entitled "Why Ecclesiology? Imagining a New Theology of Youth Ministry for the Church" by Brad Griffin and Kara Powell, available at www.fulleryouthinstitute.org, as well as from Kara Powell, "God Welcomes Children Fully into the Family of Faith," from *Understanding God's Heart for Children*, ed. Douglas McConnell, Jennifer Orona, and Paul Stockley (Colorado Springs, Colo.: World Vision, 2007).

2. As Dr. Martin Luther King Jr. declared in a 1963 speech at Western Michigan University, "We must face the fact that in America, the church is still the most segregated major institution in America. At 11:00 on Sunday morning when we stand and sing that Christ has no east or west, we stand at the most segregated hour in this nation. This is tragic." ("Dr. Martin Luther King's 1963 WMU Speech Found: Questions & Answers," Archives & Regional History Collections, Western Michigan University Libraries, http://www.wmich.edu/library/archives/mlk/q-a.html.)

3. Judith Gundry-Volf, " 'To Such as These Belongs the Reign of God': Jesus and Children," *Theology Today* 56, no. 4 (January 2000), 470. There are some negative references toward children in the Old Testament, such as Elisha's calling down a curse on children who were jeering at him (2 Kings 2:23-24) and the reference to the "folly" which is "bound up in the heart of a child" (Proverbs 22:15a). However, in general children were

viewed positively, so much so that Jews could fathom that the long-awaited Messiah would be born as a baby (Isaiah 7:14). (Robin Maas, "Christ as The Logos of Childhood: Reflections on the Meaning and Mission of the Child," *Theology Today* 56, no. 4 [January 2000], 458–459).

4. Bonnie J. Miller-McLemore, *Let the Children Come: Reimagining Childhood from a Christian Perspective* (San Francisco: Jossey-Bass, 2003), 96-98.

5. Dionysius of Halicarnassus *Rom. Ant.* 2.26.4, as quoted in Judith M. Gundry-Volf, "The Least and the Greatest," *The Child in Christian Thought*, ed. Marcia J. Bunge (Grand Rapids, Mich.: Eerdmans, 2001), 33.

6. Gundry-Volf, "The Least and the Greatest," 34.

7. Keith White, "Rediscovering Children at the Heart of Mission," *Celebrating Children*, ed. Glenn Miles and Josephine-Joy Wright (Carlisle, Cumbria, U.K.: Paternoster Press, 2003), 192.

8. Ibid.

9. Gundry-Volf, "To Such as These Belongs the Reign of God: Jesus and Children," 475-476.

10. Stuart Cummings-Bond, "The One-Eared Mickey Mouse," *YouthWorker* (Fall 1989), 76.

CHAPTER SEVEN

ESSENTIAL REST
TWO PRACTICES EVERY LEADER CAN TRY

ESSENTIAL THOUGHTS[1]

You might have an addiction—an addiction so secret that even *you* don't realize your dependence.

You may be steering clear of Internet pornography and drugs. You may even tell yourself that your love for caffè mochas in the morning is more about the taste than the caffeine and that your Wii obsession is just an attempt at remaining culturally relevant.

It's not external substances that are your first love; instead, it's a substance produced by your own body. Ironically, you might be addicted to adrenaline. Adrenaline addiction, while rarely discussed, is perhaps one of the more pervasive addictions for leaders and youth workers today.

Two Decades of Research

Over the last two decades, the research and writings of Fuller Seminary professor Dr. Archibald Hart have helped thousands of leaders wrestling with adrenaline addiction break through toward some answers. In his groundbreaking book, *The Hidden Link Between Adrenaline and Stress*, Hart writes—

> The lives of most of us are far too hectic and fast-paced. We are driven by a need to succeed, and a very distinctive need to prove ourselves. This leaves little room for relaxation or leisure in our hectic lives. It's as if we are trapped

on a runaway train and don't know where the brakes are. The engines of our bodies have jammed at full throttle.[2]

Hart also suggests in his book *Thrilled to Death* that today's stress levels are creating even more significant problems than when he first developed his adrenaline addiction theory 20 years ago. Hart warns—

Unless we, as a society, learn to slow down, examine our values, and change our hectic lifestyles, we will continue to suffer from cardiovascular disease, immune deficiencies, depression, and a host of other illnesses. Further, we will pass these traits and poor coping skills to our children.[3]

Two Ancient Escapes for Our Current Reality

Escape 1: A weekly Sabbath

Hart recommends a number of paths toward freedom from our adrenaline addiction, including monitoring our adrenaline arousal, conscious physical relaxation, sleep, changing our type-A thinking patterns, and even, in rare cases, medical treatment. In addition to all of these, perhaps one of the more effective escape routes for youth workers trapped in adrenaline addiction stems from one of the areas inevitably affected: Our spirituality.

This might surprise you, but we who struggle with busy schedules and adrenaline addiction can find the first of two escapes in an Old Testament book we probably don't visit too often: Leviticus. While we often dismiss Leviticus as "just a bunch of rules," these rules are enveloped in an important context: "As you do these things, remember that God is holy and you have been claimed by his love." So take a look at Leviticus 23:3: "There are six days when you may work, but the seventh day is a day of sabbath rest, a day of sacred assembly. You are not to do any work; wherever you live, it is a sabbath to the LORD."

You may be thinking, *Great. Bring on more guilt. I know this one: I'm a Sabbath-breaker!* Relax. I believe God intends this to be a word of freedom, and we're invited to claim it for our own lives—even for our youth ministries.

This freedom begins by understanding some of the early words of the Old Testament:

By the seventh day God had finished the work he had been doing; so on the seventh day he rested from all his work. Then God blessed the seventh day and made it holy, because on it he rested from all the work of creating that he had done. (Genesis 2:2-3)

The poetry of this creation account culminates not in the dramatic work of God, but in the powerful revelation that even the Creator rested. God stopped. God wasn't anxious about creation or worried about what would happen next. God was confident enough to cease—to take a *Sabbath*—and Scripture says God did this for a whole day.[4] The key here isn't whether God created in seven actual days (you can take that up with your favorite biblical scholar), but rather the radical announcement of the Genesis text: Our God does not feverishly race to do more stuff. We can have confidence in a God who boldly rests.

Escape 2: A regular prayer of *examen*

A second ancient practice we can use to help us stand against our addictive tendencies, whether they come from within or without, is the *Examen* of Consciousness. The *examen* (say it just like examine) is rooted in Ignatian spirituality and can be traced back 500 years to the founder of the "Society of Jesus" (or the Jesuits), Ignatius of Loyola.

The *examen* helps us escape our adrenaline addiction by causing us to stop and see where God has been present in our day and give thanks. Given that it generally takes about 15 minutes, it can be done anytime, anywhere, alone, or with others (your spouse, your family, the students in your youth ministry). Most often practitioners recommend doing it during the last hour before bed (a good reason to turn off your TV or computer a little earlier). There is always the danger that we'll rush through the *examen* just as we rush through the rest of our lives, so it's best if we have the time and space to settle in and focus.

Following is a schematic for the practice of *examen*:

1. **STOP AND BE PRESENT TO GOD.** The first step in the prayer of examen is to slow down, to stop, and to create some space. We allow ourselves simply to sit and be and to remember that we are in the presence of God. Once we truly stop, we take a moment and remember that we belong to God, that our days belong to God, and that our ministry and our students belong to God, too.

2. **LOOK BACK OVER TODAY WITH GRATITUDE.** Next, we ask God to illuminate the day as we prayerfully review the day's events in the light of Jesus. We remember the day with gratitude and give thanks for the gifts of this day. This review causes us to remember moments that would otherwise get lost in the midst of our adrenaline-fueled busyness. A few questions to ask ourselves include:

   > What was the "high" of my day? For what am I most grateful?

   > Where and how did God seem most present to me today?

   > What was most life-giving for me today?

   > When did I feel rested and balanced?

3. **UNCOVER THE LOWS.** As we continue to allow the Holy Spirit to illuminate our day, questions to help us better understand the low spots include:

> What was the low of my day? For what am I least grateful?

> Where did I least sense God's presence with me?

> What was the least life-giving or the most draining for me today?

> What pulled me away from being rested and balanced?

As we uncover these struggles and trials, we can commit them to God, confessing any sin and asking God to bring new life into the dark places.

4. **REST WITH GOD.** The key to the *examen* is its simplicity as a prayer of rest and reflection before God. Close your time in prayer by simply thanking God for being present with you.

One youth worker's use of the prayer of *examen*

Dr. Jude Tiersma Watson is an associate professor of urban mission at Fuller Seminary as well as a member of CRM/InnerCHANGE, a Christian Order Among the Poor, in Los Angeles. As a busy urban youth worker, the *examen* has helped her carve out the time she needs to stay centered and balanced. She writes—

In my early days in ministry, living in a busy urban center, my life often spun out of control, and I felt like I was losing touch with myself, God, and others.

A wise woman first suggested that I take time to examine my life at the end of each day by doing the *examen*. This was a difficult season in my life, and I often felt as if God was absent; practicing the *examen* gave me an opportunity to see that in fact God had been present, but I had been too preoccupied to notice. The *examen* gave me a tool to pay attention to my fast-paced life, to pay attention to where God was present, and to pay attention to myself and my responses to the events in my life.

As I examine my day, I remember those moments when I overreacted to a situation or times when I was unloving. In the presence of God's love, I can give those things to God for growth and healing and move on. While so many things around me can seem to take my life from me, in the *examen* I reclaim my life; I again *choose life*. If I am running on adrenaline, this stopping to review my day reminds me that this is not how I want to live my days, and not how I want to live my life. One of the questions that helps me do that is: "If my day has been too busy, what could I have said no to today?"

The *examen* is also a great relational tool. My husband and I use the *examen* questions to catch up with each other after a busy day—sometimes in the car, sometimes over dinner, and sometimes before going to sleep. It gives us a chance to reflect on our day with each other, as well as with ourselves. We also use it as a youth ministry tool, periodically asking groups of young people about their highs and lows for that day or that week.

Counter to a culture that endorses billboard messages such as, "You can rest when you're dead" (which I saw recently in a gym), the Sabbath and the *examen* remind us that real life doesn't come from adrenaline-hyped, action-filled lives and ministries. Real life comes from the realization that God was with us throughout the day, whether or not we realized it in certain moments. This realization may or may not bring us our next high, but it offers the true power of the Holy Spirit to sustain us and give us rest from our adrenaline addiction.

ESSENTIAL TEAM TALK

The Big Idea: As we remember who God is, we can step away from our busyness addiction and step toward essential rest.

You'll need—

> Coffee or soft drinks (something with caffeine in it)

> Chocolate

> Bibles

> Ahead of time, ask your leaders to bring their personal calendars to the meeting.

> Copies of your ministry calendar

> A copy of the DVD *The Prince of Egypt* (DreamWorks SKG, 1998) and a way to play a movie clip (a video projector, computer, or TV plus a DVD player)

> Index cards, one for each leader

> An *Essential Leadership Participant's Guide* for each of your adult volunteers

Now

Set out some coffee and chocolate for your leaders as they arrive. Before you dive into a discussion about essential rest, touch base on the action plan that your team developed during your previous team meetings. Celebrate what God and your team have done and pinpoint future next steps.

As you start your discussion, explain: **I provided chocolate and caffeine today for a specific reason—besides the fact that I like you all so much—and it's not just because we could all probably use a caffeine pick-me-up. These are two substances to which people, including maybe some of us, can become addicted. What are some other addictions people face?**

Whether or not your leaders have mentioned an addiction to a schedule or busyness, pull out your own personal calendar and invite your volunteers to turn to the Essential Team Talk section of their *Participant's Guide*. Ask:

Q: **How might your <u>schedule</u> become an addiction?**

Continue: **Over the past two decades, the research and writings of Fuller Seminary professor Dr. Archibald Hart have helped thousands of leaders wrestling with adrenaline addiction break through toward some answers.**

In his groundbreaking book *The Hidden Link Between Adrenaline and Stress*, Hart writes—

> The lives of most of us are far too hectic and fast-paced. We are driven by a need to succeed, and a very distinctive need to prove ourselves. This leaves little room for relaxation or leisure in our hectic lives. It's as if we are trapped on a runaway train and don't know where the brakes are. The engines of our bodies have jammed at full throttle.[5]

Q: **How do Hart's words relate to your own life?**

Continue: **Hart also suggests in his book *Thrilled to Death* that today's stress levels are creating even more significant problems than when he first developed his adrenaline addiction theory 20 years ago. Hart warns—**

> Unless we, as a society, learn to slow down, examine our values, and change our hectic lifestyles, we will continue to suffer from cardiovascular disease, immune deficiencies, depression, and a host of other illnesses. Further, we will pass these traits and poor coping skills to our children.[6]

Read the last sentence from the preceding quote again and then ask:

Q: **How might our own tendencies toward adrenaline addiction affect the students in our ministry?**

Q: **How do our busyness and adrenaline addictions affect our psyches? How about our relationships with others? What about our relationship with God?**

Q: **How is an addiction to adrenaline or a busy schedule similar to other addictions? How is it different?**

Point out that unlike other addictions we can physically escape (by staying out of coffeehouses or candy stores), we can't ditch our schedules.

New

Invite leaders to turn to Exodus 3 as you explain, **I once heard a talk by Louie Giglio—a talk he's given a number of places—that has changed the way I think about my schedule and adrenaline issues, as well as the way God wants to work through me.**[7]

Explain about Exodus 3—**At this point in Moses' life, God appeared to him in a burning bush and said God had heard his people, the Israelites, crying out under the oppression of the Egyptians—and God wanted to rescue them.**

Moses was probably thinking to himself, *Great. Glad to hear it!* when God did one of his typical plot twists. In Exodus 3:10, God said to Moses, "So now, go. I am sending you to Pharaoh to bring my people the Israelites out of Egypt."

Let's read Moses' response.

At this point ask for a volunteer to read aloud Exodus 3:11-14.

But Moses said to God, "Who am I that I should go to Pharaoh and bring the Israelites out of Egypt?"

And God said, "I will be with you. And this will be the sign to you that it is I who have sent you: When you have brought the people out of Egypt, you will worship God on this mountain."

Moses said to God, "Suppose I go to the Israelites and say to them, 'The God of your fathers has sent me to you,' and they ask me, 'What is his name?' Then what shall I tell them?"

God said to Moses, "I AM WHO I AM. This is what you are to say to the Israelites: 'I AM has sent me to you.' " (Exodus 3:11-14)

Then continue by saying: **Moses understandably wonders, *If they ask who sent me, what should I tell them? What's the name of the God who has sent me?* That question was extra important to Moses because in Moses' day, a name's meaning reflected the essence of a person—or in this case, a deity.**

God calls himself the great *I AM*.

Ask the group: **What words, phrases, or images enter your mind when you think of God as the *I AM*?**

After you've gotten a handful of answers, ask a rhetorical question: **If God is the great *I AM*, what does that make us?**

The great *I AM NOT*.

Think about it with me for a minute...

- **I am not our students' rescuer. God is.**
- **I am not their healer. God is.**
- **I am not their comforter. God is, through his Holy Spirit.**
- **I am not their hope, peace, or life. God is. God is. God is.**
- **And ultimately, I am not their minister. God is the ultimate shepherd.**

That brings enormous freedom to our personal lives. In the midst of students' pain and needs, WE ARE NOT the healer. God is.

How

Keep speaking: **Some of us act like the Energizer Bunny—we keep going and going and going...and to be honest, we're proud of it.**

The irony about this addiction is that we might be _workaholics_, but because we're doing good things—youth ministry—we're labeled as *dedicated* and *godly*. Plus, we tend to think that because we're committed to relational ministry, we have to build relationships with all people at all times. So we forget we need downtime—time to rest and get refilled.

As followers of Jesus, we get a special kind of rest, called _the Sabbath_.

Ask: **How many of you already have a regular Sabbath?**

Odds are good that no more than half of your team will be currently practicing the discipline of Sabbath regularly.

Continue: **It's interesting that so few of us have a Sabbath. It's one of God's original Top 10 commands for us. Let's go to Exodus 20:8. Will someone please read Exodus 20:8-11?**

> "Remember the Sabbath day by keeping it holy. Six days you shall labor and do all your work, but the seventh day is a sabbath to the LORD your God. On it you shall not do any work, neither you, nor your son or daughter, nor your male or female servant, nor your animals, nor any foreigner residing in your towns. For in six days the LORD made the heavens and the earth, the sea, and all that is in them, but he rested on the seventh day. Therefore the LORD blessed the Sabbath day and made it holy." (Exodus 20:8-11)

Continue: **Some folks think the Sabbath is an Old Testament rule that Jesus abolished. But Jesus never abolished the Sabbath. In fact, he called himself the _Lord_ of the Sabbath in Mark 2:28. Jesus abolished the _legalism_ of the Sabbath, but not the Sabbath itself.**

Now ask: **What are some of the obstacles, whether located internally in your mind or externally in your environment, that keep you from having a Sabbath?**

Field some answers, then say: **I think a big part of why we don't have a Sabbath is because we don't know what to do on a Sabbath. Those of you who do have a Sabbath, would you mind telling us what you do on that day?**

Get a few volunteers to share what they do on their Sabbaths. Then go on: **We've just heard some great ideas. I'll add another one from Eugene Peterson who describes Sabbath as a time to _pray and play_.**

It's a time to pray, meaning a time to somehow get some special time with God. And it's a time to play, meaning you do fun, unusual things you wouldn't normally do.

If you do have a regular Sabbath, it would be good for you to share what you actually do on your Sabbath.

Then continue: **Here are some other Sabbath tips to help us remember that we are the great I AM NOT:**

1. **Each week look ahead on your _calendar_ and block out some time by writing the word _Sabbath_ on it. After all, the Sabbath won't automatically appear on your calendar. You have to schedule it intentionally.**

2. **Consider a day other than _Sunday_. If you're in charge of a lot of ministry stuff on Sunday, then maybe your Sabbath could be Saturday or even a weekday.**

3. **Set aside as much time as you can, even if it's just a _half day_. There are times in my life when work demands or family commitments make an entire day of rest a bit unrealistic. On those weeks I try to set aside a half day.**

At this point have all of your leaders take out their calendars and look ahead to the next two weeks. Invite them to block off two chunks of time (ideally even two full days) during the next two weeks that they intend to use for their Sabbaths. Once your leaders have selected their blocks of time, have them write those times in their *Participant's Guide* and in their calendars and then continue with the following tips:

4. **Avoid items on your <u>to do</u> list. It's tempting to do something that is actually work (such as cleaning your garage, buying a birthday gift for your brother, sorting your clothes) on your Sabbath day. As much as possible, try to stick to activities that truly refresh and restore you. Keep reminding yourself that you've got the other six days to do everything else.**

At this point have the team write the answer to this question in their *Participant's Guide*:

Q: **What would you like to do on your next Sabbath?**

If you have time, invite your team to share some answers aloud. Then transition toward the end of the training by saying: **Let's look at how Steven Spielberg and DreamWorks depict Moses' realization that God is the great I AM.**

Play the movie clip from *The Prince of Egypt*. Start at 42:57 into the movie, just past the start of scene 15 as Moses is chasing one sheep, and end at 47:36 when Moses picks up his staff.

After the clip, ask: **How is Moses' response to God similar to our own?** *(Moses makes excuses. He claims the people won't believe him or they'll hate him because of how he used to oppress them as Pharaoh's son.)*

How does God respond to these excuses?

Transition back to your group: **In addition to looking at our need for rest in our personal lives, let's also think about our need for rest in our ministry. Let's look at our upcoming ministry calendars and see if we think this ministry schedule will allow us, as well as our students and their parents, to get the rest we all need.**

Have More Time?

Review the description of the prayer of *examen* found in the Essential Thoughts section of this chapter in the *Leader's Guide* and the *Participant's Guide*. Take 15 minutes to walk through a prayer of *examen* with your leadership team to wrap up your discussion about rest. You can invite your leaders to experience this prayer individually, in small groups, or together as a team.

Essential Rest Action Plan

Our team's ideas for how to move forward into essential rest include:

OVERALL GOALS	ACTION STEPS TOWARD THESE GOALS	SPECIFIC PRAYER REQUESTS	SIGNS OF GOD'S ACTIVITY

Distribute copies of your ministry calendar and evaluate how "rest-full" it is.

Q: **What might we want to consider eliminating either from this calendar or other calendars in the future?**

Q: **What would our students lose if we did this? What might they gain?**

Invite your leaders to turn to the Essential Rest Action Plan in their *Participant's Guide* and use its rows as a way to pinpoint specific goals, action steps, and prayer requests.

Give your leaders some time to close in prayer in pairs or small groups. If possible, have them cluster in similar life stages (single adults, young marrieds, married with kids) and share how they would like this discussion to have an impact on their lives in the next week.

At the end of the prayer time, distribute index cards and ask each person to write I AM on an index card. Then have each team member exchange index cards with someone else and use that index card as a reminder of God's I AM-ness, as well as a reminder to pray for the other teammate.

ENDNOTES: CHAPTER SEVEN

Essential Rest: Two Practices Every Leader Can Try

1. This section is a adapted from two articles entitled "R-E-S-T: The Four Letter Word of Youth Workers" by Brad Griffin and "Adrenaline: Our Secret Addiction" by Jude Tiersma Watson and Kara Powell, available at www.fulleryouthinstitute.org. "Adrenaline" was also published in the September/October 2008 issue of *The Journal of Student Ministries*, © DevelopMinistries, www.developministries.com. Used with permission.

2. Archibald D. Hart, *The Hidden Link Between Adrenaline and Stress: The Exciting New Breakthrough That Helps You Overcome Stress Damage* (Dallas: Word Publishing, 1995), 4.

3. Archibald D. Hart, *Thrilled to Death: How the Endless Pursuit of Pleasure Is Leaving Us Numb* (Nashville: Thomas Nelson, 2007), 62.

4. Walter Brueggemann, *Genesis (Interpretation: A Bible Commentary for Teaching and Preaching)*, ed. James L. Mays, Patrick D. Miller, and Paul J. Achtemeier (Atlanta: John Knox Press, 1982), 35.

5. Hart, *The Hidden Link*, 4.

6. Hart, *Thrilled to Death*, 62.

7. Louie Giglio's understanding of God's "I AM-ness" is also well-described in his book *I Am Not But I Know I AM: Welcome to the Story of God* (Sisters, Ore.: Multnomah Publishers, 2005).

CHAPTER EIGHT

ESSENTIAL HOLISTIC MINISTRY
WHOLE MINISTRY FOR THE WHOLE KID

ESSENTIAL THOUGHTS[1]

On a scale of 1 to 10, how strongly do you agree with the following statement: "If a kid can't read, it's the church's job to help him read"?

Twenty years ago, I would have been at about a two. I thought teaching a kid to read was the job of that kid's school or parents. Now I'm at about a nine, and my own church offers after-school tutoring.

What's changed? I want students to experience Jesus now more than ever. It's just that I now also want them to experience the full life that Jesus offers in this life as well as the next.

Holistic Shalom

From the very beginning God's plan has been to establish his shalom (pronounced "sha-lome") over all creation. The word *shalom* in Scripture is commonly translated as "peace." But with that meaning, we tend to reduce it to one of two inadequate definitions: Either we think of it as the absence of war and conflict, or we view it as an individual subjective sense of well-being.

In reality biblical shalom is far more than just a lack of fighting or a warm and fuzzy feeling. In describing shalom and its relationship to ministry, Nicholas Wolterstorff from Yale University writes, "The state of *shalom* is the state of flourishing in all dimensions of one's existence: in one's relation to God, in one's relation to one's fellow human beings, in one's relation to nature, and in one's relation to oneself."[2]

God's shalom is an all-inclusive peace encompassing our whole selves and all of our relationships—with God, with self, with others, and with the world. When humanity fell into sin, that sense of well-being was broken, leaving in its wake darkness, pain, and death. Yet despite our rebellion and the sin-filled consequences that have left the whole of creation "groaning" (Romans 8:22), God's commitment to restore shalom hasn't wavered.

So if a child can't read or a community is plagued with violence or public schools are deteriorating, offering a Bible study is a start—but it's not all we can offer.

If we want teenagers to experience true shalom, we can offer them a holistic youth ministry that also helps them grow relationally, emotionally, mentally, and socially.

Holistic Ministry Through the Assets

The Search Institute, a well-known research center in Minnesota, is a valuable resource to help us expose our students to the holistic shalom God intends. Based on surveys with nearly 3 million youth in the United States and Canada since 1989, the Search Institute has developed the 40 Developmental Assets. These assets represent 40 building blocks of development available through our surrounding communities and relationships that help people of all ages (including teenagers) thrive.

Half the assets are *external* and focus on what students receive from others. They fall under the categories of Support, Empowerment, Boundaries and Expectations, and Constructive Use of Time. The remaining half of the assets are *internal* and are also divided into four categories: Commitment to Learning, Positive Values, Social Competencies, and Positive Identity.[3] To read a list of the 40 Developmental Assets, turn to page 100.

We who long for essential holistic ministry must pay attention to these assets and their power in our students' lives. Research indicates that the more assets a teenager possesses, the more likely she is to exhibit leadership, maintain good health, value diversity, and succeed in school. In contrast the fewer assets a kid possesses, the more likely he is to use alcohol and drugs, be sexually active, and commit acts of violence.

Assets evident in 30 percent or less of the teenagers surveyed include the following:

> Positive family communication (asset 2)

> Caring school climate (asset 5)

> Community values youth (asset 7)

> Youth as resources (asset 8)

> Adult role models (asset 14)

> Creative activities (asset 17)

> Reading for pleasure (asset 25)

> Planning and decision making (asset 32)

The Search Institute also reports that many of the assets are evident in 60 percent or more of the teens they surveyed, including—

> Family support (asset 1)

> Positive peer influence (asset 15)

> Religious community (asset 19)

> Achievement motivation (asset 21)

> School engagement (asset 22)

> Integrity (asset 28)

> Honesty (asset 29)

> Responsibility (asset 30)

> Positive view of personal future (asset 40)

Much of what we typically value in youth ministry is represented in the 40 assets. Relationship with Jesus and involvement in church are reflected in asset 19, religious community, which means a student is spending one or more hours a week in religious activities. The common youth ministry value of adult mentoring is specifically represented in asset 14, adult role models. Some youth ministries, especially those serving urban youth, also work diligently to boost students' educational experience, which is represented by school engagement (asset 22) and doing at least one hour of homework every school day (asset 23).

Yet other assets exist that many of us don't generally consider as we try to love and serve students. These include a caring neighborhood (asset 4), caring school climate (asset 5), creative activities (asset 17), cultural competence (asset 34), and peaceful conflict resolution (asset 36). Helping teenagers escape pain-filled homes, schools, and neighborhoods—or even just helping them through the common ups and downs of adolescence—means we need to think about how some of those assets that seem outside of the scope of our youth ministries might be surprisingly important in students' growth and transformation.

Applying the 40 Assets to Real-Life Youth Ministry

Youth ministries in the United States that take seriously an asset-based approach tend to find that the assets shape their ministries in four primary ways.

1. MINISTRY PROGRAMS AND PHILOSOPHY. At a fundamental level, asset-sensitive youth ministries tend to redesign their ministry programs to ensure that assets are developed every time they gather with students. Often this means minor tweaks or nuances to existing programs. The traditional senior banquet is turned into a more intentional night of blessing and honoring for seniors to reinforce their awareness that the community deeply values and cares for them (asset 7). Cross-cultural mission trips are planned with an eye to enhancing students' planning and decision making (asset 32), interpersonal competence (asset 33), cultural competence (asset 34), resistance skills (asset 35), and peaceful conflict resolution (asset 36). Parent meetings can become opportunities to build assets such as 2, positive family communication. And as you weave students into music and other creative arts in your ministry, you build the creative activities described by asset 17.

2. CURRICULUM DEVELOPMENT. Given the power of the assets in teenagers' lives, some youth ministries have used the developmental assets as a framework for teaching and curriculum development so students are explicitly trained in how to embody the assets.

Those ministries have asked, "Where, if at all, does this asset show itself in Scripture?" and then crafted an asset-oriented teaching series along with other important theological topics.

For instance, one asset most youth ministries would affirm is family support (asset 1). So where does family support surface in Scripture? We immediately see in Genesis what happens when family systems tragically break down in the stories of Cain and Abel and Jacob and Esau (Genesis 4 and 25). We see God's charge to the Israelite community in raising children in Deuteronomy 6:4-9. We see themes of abandonment, adoption, and redemption in the stories of Moses, Samuel, and Eli (Exodus and 1 Samuel 3). Jesus speaks to the nature and composition of family (Mathew 10). And Paul gives instructions to parents and families in several of his books (Ephesians 6:4, Colossians 3:21, and 1 Timothy 5).

A second example is equality and social justice (asset 27). We could begin in Genesis with the Tower of Babel (11:1-9), teach about the Year of Jubilee in Leviticus (chapter 25), pick up any of the prophets, or highlight Jesus' own words about caring for "the least of these" (Matthew 25:40-45). Teaching in this manner is not only true to the whole Bible, but also helps your students become more whole through your teaching.

3. VOLUNTEER RECRUITMENT. Youth ministries who shift to an asset-based model tend to find that their leadership pool increases exponentially. Regardless of age, gender, occupation, or education, almost every adult in the community is a potential volunteer leader because almost every adult can help develop and nurture at least one asset in a student's life. The question behind recruitment begins to shift from, "Do we have enough leaders?" to "How can we all use our unique contributions to build assets into the lives of our students?"

4. ADVOCACY. Beautiful things can happen when God's people come together and say the same thing at the same time, whether lifting our voices in song, responding together in prayer, or collectively advocating for what we believe to be true and best. The 40 Developmental Assets can help churches and youth ministries know how to use their collective voices to advocate for students. Whether applied during the parent-training seminars, through the encouragement of public school administrators and influence on the policies they create, or in the way ministries work alongside local authorities to decide how best to use grant funding, the developmental assets can give our youth ministries common language and common goals that enhance our partnerships with public schools and other community-based organizations.

So now what do you think? If a kid can't read, is it the church's job to help him read—or at least to partner with other organizations that can help? The shalom I want for my own three children, the students in our youth ministry, and the teens in my community leads me to answer yes.

ESSENTIAL TEAM TALK

The Big Idea: We can play a part in meeting not just students' spiritual needs, but also their physical, emotional, social, and intellectual needs.

You'll need—

> Whiteboard or poster paper

> Markers

> Five pieces of paper with one of the following phrases listed as a header on each: PHYSICAL NEEDS, EMOTIONAL NEEDS, SOCIAL NEEDS, SPIRITUAL NEEDS, and INTELLECTUAL NEEDS

> Pens

> Bibles

> An *Essential Leadership Participant's Guide* for each of your adult volunteers

Now

Greet your adult volunteers and touch base on the action plans your team developed during your previous team meetings. Celebrate what God and your team have done and pinpoint future next steps.

Transition the focus to essential holistic ministry by announcing that you're going to begin with a short true-false test. In response to the inevitable moans and groans, tell them that when you say a short test, you mean a *very* short test. In fact, this test has only two questions.

True or False: All teenagers need Jesus.

Have your volunteers share their answers and explain why they answered as they did.

True or False: All that students need is Jesus.

Again, have your volunteers share their answers and their reasoning.

Divide your adult volunteers into five different teams (or if you have fewer than five volunteers, simply have each person be her own team). Give each team one of the five pieces of paper labeled with the various types of needs and 30 seconds to write as many needs of teenagers that fit into that category as they can. Then have them pass their paper to the team on their left. Give the teams another 30 seconds to read the needs already listed and try to write any additional needs for that category. Continue until you've done five different rounds.

Next ask whoever is holding each paper to read the needs listed. After all five papers have been read, invite your leaders to turn to the Essential Team Talk of their *Participant's Guide* and ask:

Q: **What were your thoughts and feelings as you heard the diverse needs of students?**

Hold up the paper labeled SPIRITUAL NEEDS and ask:

Q: **Which of our students' spiritual needs should we be concerned about?**

Odds are good that your adult volunteers will say your team should be concerned about most, if not all, of them. Then hold up the other four papers and ask:

Q: **Which of these other needs should we also be concerned about? Please explain your answer.**

Q: **Some youth workers believe that youth ministries should focus on teenagers' spiritual needs and let other people and groups (families, schools, community organizations) take care of the rest. How would you respond to that belief?**

Q: **How do you think Jesus might respond to a youth ministry that follows this belief?**

Continue: **We can get a sense for how Jesus might respond from the way he responded to a paralyzed man in Mark 2:1-12. Let's read the passage together.**

For variety's sake you may want to ask for two volunteers to read the story—one leader reads Jesus' words while the other one reads everything else.

A few days later, when Jesus again entered Capernaum, the people heard that he had come home. They gathered in such large numbers that there was no room left, not even outside the door, and he preached the word to them. Some men came, bringing to him a paralyzed man, carried by four of them. Since they could not get him to Jesus because of the crowd, they made an opening in the roof above Jesus by digging through it and then lowered the mat the man was lying on. When Jesus saw their faith, he said to the paralyzed man, "Son, your sins are forgiven."

Now some teachers of the law were sitting there, thinking to themselves, "Why does this fellow talk like that? He's blaspheming! Who can forgive sins but God alone?"

Immediately Jesus knew in his spirit that this was what they were thinking in their hearts, and he said to them, "Why are you thinking these things? Which is easier: to say to this paralyzed man, 'Your sins are forgiven,' or to say, 'Get up, take your mat and walk'? But I want you to know that the Son of Man has authority on earth to forgive sins." So he said to the man, "I tell you, get up, take your mat and go home." He got up, took his mat and walked out in full view of them all. This amazed everyone and they praised God, saying, "We have never seen anything like this!" (Mark 2:1-12)

After the reading say: **Homes in first-century Palestine were different than most of our homes today. A typical peasant's house was a small, one-room structure with a flat roof. In some homes an outside staircase may have led to the roof. The roof itself was usually made of wooden beams covered with thatch and compacted earth to keep rain and moisture from entering the house. Sometimes tiles were laid between the beams and thatch for even greater protection.**

In this passage the four men, upon seeing how crowded the one-room house was, probably carried the paralyzed man up the outside staircase, dug through the thatch and earth, and lowered him between the beams.

Q: **In Mark 2:1-12 does Jesus choose to help this man's soul or his body?** *(The answer is both.)*

Q: **Do you think there's any significance to the fact that Jesus forgave the man's sins before healing him? Why or why not?**

New

Explain: **The Search Institute, a well-known research center in Minnesota, can help us think about how to care for even more of students' needs than we currently do. Based on surveys with nearly 3 million youth in the United States and Canada since 1989, the Search Institute has developed the 40 Developmental Assets—40 building blocks of development available through our surrounding communities and relationships to help people of all ages, including teenagers, thrive.**

At this point invite your team to turn to the 40 Developmental Assets table in their *Participant's Guide* as you continue your explanation. For easy reference your own list of the assets follows.

The 40 Developmental Assets® for Adolescents (Ages 12-18)

External Assets

CATEGORY	ASSET NAME AND DEFINITION
Support	1. Family Support—Family life provides high levels of love and support.
	2. Positive Family Communication—Young person and her or his parent(s) communicate positively, and young person is willing to seek advice and counsel from parents.
	3. Other Adult Relationships—Young person receives support from three or more nonparent adults.
	4. Caring Neighborhood—Young person experiences caring neighbors.
	5. Caring School Climate—School provides a caring, encouraging environment.
	6. Parent Involvement in Schooling—Parent(s) are actively involved in helping the child succeed in school.
Empowerment	7. Community Values Youth—Young person perceives that adults in the community value youth.
	8. Youth as Resources—Young people are given useful roles in the community.
	9. Service to Others—Young person serves in the community one hour or more per week.
	10. Safety—young person feels safe at home, at school, and in the neighborhood.
Boundaries and Expectations	11. Family Boundaries—Family has clear rules and consequences and monitors the young person's whereabouts.
	12. School Boundaries—School provides clear rules and consequences.
	13. Neighborhood Boundaries—Neighbors take responsibility for monitoring young people's behavior.
	14. Adult Role Models—Parent(s) and other adults model positive, responsible behavior.
	15. Positive Peer Influence—Young person's best friends model responsible behavior.
	16. High Expectations—Both parent(s) and teachers encourage the young person to do well.
Constructive Use of Time	17. Creative Activities—Young person spends three or more hours per week in lessons or practice in music, theater, or other arts.
	18. Youth Programs—Young person spends three or more hours per week in sports, clubs, or organizations at school and/or in community.
	19. Religious Community—Young person spends one hour or more per week in activities in a religious institution.
	20. Time at Home—Young person is out with friends "with nothing special to do" two or fewer nights per week.

The 40 Developmental Assets® for Adolescents (Ages 12-18)

Internal Assets

CATEGORY	ASSET NAME AND DEFINITION
Commitment to Learning	21. Achievement Motivation—Young person is motivated to do well in school.
	22. School Engagement—Young person is actively engaged in learning.
	23. Homework—Young person reports doing at least one hour of homework every school day.
	24. Bonding to School—Young person cares about her or his school.
	25. Reading for Pleasure—Young person reads for pleasure three or more hours per week.
Positive Values	26. Caring—Young person places high value on helping other people.
	27. Equality and Social Justice—Young person places high value on promoting equality and reducing hunger and poverty.
	28. Integrity—Young person acts on convictions and stands up for her or his beliefs.
	29. Honesty—Young person "tells the truth even when it is not easy."
	30. Responsibility—Young person accepts and takes personal responsibility.
	31. Restraint—Young person believes it is important not to be sexually active or to use alcohol or other drugs.
Social Competencies	32. Planning and Decision Making—Young person knows how to plan ahead and make choices.
	33. Interpersonal Competence—Young person has empathy, sensitivity, and friendship skills.
	34. Cultural Competence—Young person has knowledge of and comfort with people of different cultural/racial/ethnic backgrounds.
	35. Resistance Skills—Young person can resist negative peer pressure and dangerous situations.
	36. Peaceful Conflict Resolution—Young person seeks to resolve conflict nonviolently.
Positive Identity	37. Personal Power—Young person feels he or she has control over "things that happen to me."
	38. Self-Esteem—Young person reports having a high self-esteem.
	39. Sense of Purpose—Young person reports that "my life has a purpose."
	40. Positive View of Personal Future—Young person is optimistic about her or his personal future

Continue: **As you can see, half of the assets are *external* and focus on what teens receive from others. They fall under the categories of support, empowerment, boundaries and expectations, and constructive use of time.**

The remaining half of the assets are *internal* and reflect the four constructs of commitment to learning, positive values, social competencies, and positive identity.

We who long for essential holistic ministry can't afford to ignore these assets and their power in our students' lives.

Research indicates that the more assets kids possess, the more likely they are to exhibit leadership, maintain good health, value diversity, and succeed in school. In contrast, the fewer assets teens possess, the more likely they are to use alcohol and drugs, be sexually active, and commit acts of violence.

Q: **In addition to promoting positive growth and avoiding these types of risky behaviors, how do you think having more assets would affect our students' relationships with Jesus?**

Q: **How many assets would you guess the average sixth to 12th grader in the United States has?** *(The answer is 19.3 assets.)*[4]

Q: **In general, would you guess that older teenagers have more or fewer assets than younger teenagers do?** *(The answer is fewer.)*

Q: **Would you guess that boys have more or fewer assets than girls do? Why is that?** *(The answer is fewer.)*

Have More Time?

Help your team think about the power of the assets in their lives by asking them to read the list of assets and circle those that were evident in their own lives as teenagers. Invite your volunteers to share about one or two assets that were especially formative during their own teenage ups and downs.

Continue: **Although there is no magic number of assets that guarantees teenagers will thrive, the Search Institute hints that _31_ assets is a common benchmark dividing students who do well from those who struggle. Yet only _8_ percent of the youth they've surveyed have 31 or more assets. (And more than half have 20 or fewer assets.)**[5]

Q: **What does 8 percent tell you about our own students?**

On your whiteboard, draw two concentric circles. Label the inner circle: PROVIDE and the outer circle PARTNER WITH.

Give your volunteers time to read slowly over the assets list and invite them to put a star next to any asset that your ministry can provide and a check mark next to any asset you could provide if you partnered with another individual or organization (such as schools, churches, community-based organizations).

When they're finished, have them share their answers. As they share, you can write either the asset numbers or a brief one- to two-word description of the asset in the circles you've drawn.

Next ask:

Q: **Looking at the list of assets that we think we can provide, which one or two should we focus on with our students in the next six months?**

Q: **Now looking at the list of assets we could provide if we partner with others, which one or two should we focus on in the next six months?**

Q: **Who else could we partner with (parents, schools, other community-based organizations, or churches) who could enhance our influence over these assets?**

How

At this point invite your leaders to turn to a copy of the following Student-Asset Wish List table in their *Participant's Guide* and have them write down the names of two to three kids in the spaces given. Invite them to write down two to five assets they would like to see developed in each specific kid.

Student-Asset Wish List

NAME OF STUDENT	ASSET TO BE DEVELOPED

After everyone has finished filling in this chart, ask them to share their answers. Then continue with these questions:

Q: **What themes did you see in the assets we wrote down as a team?**

Q: **What can we in this room do to instill those assets we've just discussed in our students?**

Q: **Imagine that we viewed our role not just as asset providers, but as recruiters of other asset providers. Who do we know in our community, our neighborhood, or our church who can help build these essential assets in our kids?** Use leaders' responses as an opportunity to affirm the importance of parents, relatives, teachers, coaches, neighbors, family friends, and other church members in providing resources for your students.

Invite your leaders to turn to the Essential Holistic Ministry Action Plan in their *Participant's Guide* and use its rows as a way to pinpoint specific goals, action steps, and prayer requests.

Close in prayer by asking your volunteers to get into two groups. One group will pray for the assets over which your ministry can provide, and the other group will pray for the assets you can provide through partnerships. As appropriate, pray also for specific students and ask God to give you eyes to see all the diverse ways your ministry can help surround students with the assets they need to thrive.

Have More Time?

Brainstorm simple ways to thank the adults who are investing in your kids, such as writing notes to coaches or bringing doughnuts to local teachers. Choose one or two of your ideas and enlist a few students in implementing them in the next few months.

Essential Holistic Ministry Action Plan

Our team's ideas for how to move forward into essential holistic ministry include:

OVERALL GOALS	ACTION STEPS TOWARD THESE GOALS	SPECIFIC PRAYER REQUESTS	SIGNS OF GOD'S ACTIVITY

ENDNOTES: CHAPTER EIGHT

Essential Holistic Ministry: Whole Ministry for the Whole Kid

1. This section is adapted from an article entitled "Turning Toward Holistic Ministry" by Mark Maines, available at www.fulleryouthinstitute.org, as well as from chapter 5 of *Deep Ministry in a Shallow World* (Grand Rapids, Mich.: Zondervan/Youth Specialties, 2006) and chapter 5 of *Deep Justice in a Broken World* (Grand Rapids, Mich.: Zondervan/ Youth Specialties, 2008), both coauthored by Chap Clark and Kara Powell.

2. Nicholas Wolterstorff, "The Contours of Justice: An Ancient Call for *Shalom*," in *God and the Victim: Theological Reflections on Evil, Victimization, Justice, and Forgiveness*, ed. Lisa Barnes Lampman and Michelle D. Shattuck (Grand Rapids, Mich.: Eerdmans, 1999), 113.

3. To peruse more asset-based resources developed by the Search Institute, go to www. search-institute.org. You could also check out Peter Benson's *All Kids Are Our Kids: What Communities Must Do to Raise Caring and Responsible Children and Adolescents*, 2nd ed. (San Francisco: Jossey-Bass, 2006).

4. "How Many Assets Do Young People Have?" Search Institute,

   http://www.search-institute.org/research/assets/asset-levels.

5. Ibid.

CHAPTER NINE

ESSENTIAL IMPACT
FAITH BEYOND HIGH SCHOOL

ESSENTIAL THOUGHTS[1]

We all have our Nicoles.

Nicole was in my small group from her ninth-grade year until she graduated. Of the seven girls in the group, Nicole was the most loud, the most provocative, and to be honest, the most fun. I could always count on Nicole to liven up our discussions with questions such as, "Do I have to be nice to people who totally annoy me?" and "Does it hurt to have sex?"

I did all the normal small group stuff with Nicole and the other girls. We had overnighters at my house. We went toilet papering. We'd grab lunch after church. We talked about everything from guys to grace to getting braces.

When Nicole walked across the stage on June 16 to receive her high school diploma, I couldn't have been more proud. I felt as though my own little sister in the Lord was graduating.

I'd spent four years with Nicole, but I had given absolutely zero thought to June 17. Or July 17. Or August 17. My job—or so I thought—was to get her across the finish line of high school graduation.

So what happened after June 16? Following graduation, Nicole stopped coming to our church worship services. Soon after that she stopped returning my calls. I had a new flock of ninth graders in front of me, so I stopped leaving her messages. Every few months when I thought of Nicole, I'd toss up a "God, please keep her close to you" prayer, but I wasn't sure I'd ever see her again.

Eighteen months later I ran into Nicole while I was doing some shopping. She wasn't alone. She was pushing a stroller. After we hugged, she somewhat timidly introduced me to her nine-month-old daughter and told me she had lost contact with her daughter's father. When I asked her if she ever went to church, she said she wasn't into "that God stuff" anymore.

While I was thrilled to see her, our conversation was dripping with awkwardness. We had shared four years of life together. We had talked about Jesus and what it meant to follow him for our whole lives. Now we both stood there feeling guilty—Nicole because she had a daughter and not a husband, and me because I had failed to follow up with Nicole after she graduated.

As I drove from the mall back to church, I couldn't help but wonder: What had I done wrong as a small group leader? What conversations with Nicole could I have handled better? What should I have done in Nicole's life but didn't?

We all have our Nicoles.

We all have students who graduate from our youth ministry and seem to graduate from following God as well.

We all have students who walk the narrow path in high school but then somehow make a U-turn and stumble—or maybe even sprint—in the opposite direction.

Because of the growing national concern over students like Nicole, we at the Fuller Youth Institute have launched the College Transition Project to study more than 400 youth group graduates during their first three years in college.[2] In the most recent study, our initial surveys reveal that during graduates' freshman years, 44 percent significantly or moderately agree that "my college environment is helping me grow as a Christian," while 29 percent moderately or significantly disagree. Somewhat similarly, 42 percent of the students we've surveyed moderately or significantly disagree that "it's been difficult to find a church where I feel welcome," while 29 percent moderately or strongly agree.

While we aren't yet finished with our study, this data (along with findings in parallel studies) seems to suggest that about 40 to 50 percent of students in youth groups struggle with their faith after graduation.

What distinguishes those students whose faith thrives in college from those who are struggling to survive? What can our youth ministries do now—before students graduate—to put them on a trajectory of lifelong faith after the "Pomp and Circumstance" fades?

Looking in the Mirror

As those two questions are analyzed through our College Transition Project, we are discovering that the answers are far from simple. In the flood of data we're swimming through, one consistent theme emerges: We should not underestimate the importance of our role as youth leaders in students' faith development.

Why do you go to youth group?

When 200 of our students were still high school seniors, we asked them to rank the reasons they came to youth group. Many of us probably would have expected "friends" to be the number one answer. So we were surprised by the responses, which are listed in the following table in order of importance:

Why Do You Go to Youth Group?

RANKING	ITEM
1	Like my youth pastor
2	Learn about God there
3	Feel comfortable there
4	Can really worship God
5	Have always gone
6	Experience real fellowship
7	Learn to serve
8	Reinforces what I believe
9	Helps me grow spiritually
10	Feels like real community
11	It's fun
12	Feel like I belong
13	Like youth pastor's sermons
14	Learn the Bible
15	Safe to talk to peers about doubts and questions
16	Safe to talk to adults about doubts and questions
17	Where my friends are
18	Adults take time to really listen
19	Parents encourage me to go
20	Escape from the world
21	Feel guilty if I don't go
22	Parents make me go

Contrary to what many of us might have guessed, students' connections with their youth workers are more important than their connections with their friends. While we're pleased that they have such a strong bond with us as adult leaders, we can't help but ask: Given the rocky transitions that students often face when they leave our ministries, is it possible they have become too dependent on us?

How would you describe your relationships with your youth leaders?

We asked youth group graduates during their first year in college to reflect on their relationships with their youth leaders. More than 50 percent of those surveyed described the statements in the following table as "very true" or "completely true" about their youth leaders.

How Would You Describe Your Relationships with Your Youth Leaders?

QUALITY	PERCENTAGE OF YOUTH GROUP GRADUATES WHO BELIEVED THIS WAS "VERY TRUE" OR "COMPLETELY TRUE"
They cared about me as a person.	87.2%
They were interested in my life.	69.4%
They took time to really listen to me.	67.5%
They stood by me.	67.5%
They gave me guidance.	66.3%
I felt I could trust them with my personal issues.	61.8%
I didn't feel judged by them.	58.6%
They helped me to realistically apply my faith to daily life.	58.0%
They sought me out.	50.4%

Interestingly, two attributes ranked dramatically lower than the rest. The first was "Their lives were positive examples of Christian spirituality," which was marked by 38.9 percent of students as "very true" or "completely true." The second was "I felt like they really knew me," which was "very true" or "completely true" for just 29.7 percent of youth group graduates. So while we have much to celebrate in our relationships with our upperclassmen, those of us who want to move into more essential leadership should ask: *What type of Christian spirituality are we modeling? And are students showing us the good, the bad, and the ugly of who they really are, or are we seeing only the cleaned-up, "Sunday school" versions?*

How comfortable do students feel sharing their doubts and struggles?

One of the themes that emerged repeatedly in our interviews is that in their later years in high school, as well as during their early college years, students are confronted with new questions about their faith and worldview. Yet in the midst of these new questions, students aren't sure where to go for answers or even for a safe place for discussion.

It's not clear whether their relationships with us are providing that safety. Almost 69 percent of youth group graduates reported that they had wanted to talk to their youth leaders about doubt while they were still in high school, but only 48.3 percent actually did so. Yet when seniors did talk with their adult leaders about their doubts, 74.7 percent reported that it was helpful.

Findings like these can help us move into essential leadership by prodding us to ask ourselves: *What is it about us that might make students think we're not safe people for them to share their doubts with? When a student does talk with us about their doubts and struggles, what do we do well? What should we be doing differently?*

What happens to kids' relationships with us after graduation?

The short answer is this: Those relationships plummet. More than 22 percent of freshmen who were youth group kids report "never" having contact with a youth leader after graduation, and an additional 34.4 percent are in touch once a month or less. In the fall of their freshman year, students report that if they need emotional support, only 17.8 percent would "definitely" contact a former youth leader.

Youth workers face the difficult challenge that spring not only brings senior graduation, but also delivers a new crop of eager-but-intimidated ninth graders (not to mention their parents). Yet as we balance the needs of our old students with the needs of our new students, we can ask ourselves: *In an era of evolving communication systems, what social networking venues or technologies can we use to stay in better touch with students? How can we help our current students keep in touch with our graduates?* Answering those questions not only helps our graduates, but also communicates to our current students that we won't forget about them when they leave.

My Nicole...and Your Nicole, Too

As I've analyzed this data and talked with youth group graduates, I can't help but think about Nicole. I did a lot well in my relationship with her, but I also wish I could redo a lot. As someone who wants to be a more essential leader, I'm no longer satisfied with only about half of our students thriving in their faith after high school.

I care too much about kids—my students and your students—to be satisfied with 50 percent. I care too much about the kingdom to be satisfied with 50 percent. And in all honesty, I work too hard in youth ministry to be satisfied with 50 percent. Don't you?

ESSENTIAL TEAM TALK

The Big Idea: By taking essential strategic steps now, we can help our students' faith flourish after they graduate from our ministries.

You'll need—

> A copy of the song "Pomp and Circumstance" and a way to play it (CD or MP3 player)

> A copy of the "Connect for Life" video clip available at www.fulleryouthinstitute.org and a way to play it (video projector, computer, or DVD player and a TV)

> Copies of a list containing the names of your seniors

> An *Essential Leadership Participant's Guide* for each of your adult volunteers

Now

Greet your staff and touch base on the action plans that your team developed during your previous team meetings. Celebrate what God and your team have done and pinpoint future next steps.

Help your leaders get in touch with what it's like to be a graduating senior by playing the "Pomp and Circumstance" song. Listen in silence for 15 to 20 seconds and then invite your leaders to turn to Essential Team Talk in their *Participant's Guide*.

Explain: **You'll find a Seniors' Feelings table with four quadrants marked Mad, Glad, Sad, and Scared. As we continue to listen to "Pomp and Circumstance," take a few minutes to write down the ways our graduating seniors might be feeling mad, glad, sad, or scared.**

Seniors' Feelings

Glad

Mad

Scared

Sad

After giving your leaders a few minutes to write students' emotions, invite them to share their ideas.

Then ask: **What other emotions did you think our graduating seniors might be experiencing?**

Explain: **As the Essential Thoughts article indicates, about half of the students from our youth ministry are likely to experience significant faith struggles when they graduate. A ministry coalition called the Youth Transition Network recently interviewed college students around the country to better understand all they'll face after the "Pomp and Circumstance" fades. I'm going to play a five-minute video clip, and as you watch this clip, please keep in mind that all of these college students are youth group graduates.**

Play the video clip and then ask: **What in this video confirms what you might have suspected? What surprises you?**

New

Continue: **Our Essential Thoughts article for this study describes some of the data from the College Transition Project at the Fuller Youth Institute. Let's take a few minutes to look more closely at four additional findings from this three-year study of youth group graduates.**

Finding 1: High school students who _refrained_ from sex and alcohol let loose in college.

This probably won't shock you, but our youth group graduates will drink more alcohol and have more sexual encounters in college than they did in high school. But here's a surprising twist: The students who have the highest rates of increase in alcohol and sex were those who *abstained in high school*. I should clarify that even though the former teetotalers have a more dramatic *increase* in those two risky behaviors, their overall rates of alcohol use and sexual encounters are still lower than youth group graduates who were drinking and having sex during high school.

    Q: What, if anything, does this tell you about the faith of those teetotalers?

    Q: What thoughts or questions does this finding raise about our youth ministry?

Finding 2: The value of _leadership_ roles

Youth group graduates who were involved in leadership roles in their churches—whether in the youth ministry or in other areas of the church, such as junior high or children's ministry—seem to have a more mature faith during their first year in college. Ask—

    Q: Why do you think this is the case?

    Q: What are the implications for how we interact with students who aren't in official leadership roles?

Finding 3: Involvement in the _larger church_ makes a difference.

In addition to leadership roles, one of the other factors most highly correlated with faith maturity in students' college freshman year was participation in all-church worship services during high school.

    Q: Why do you think all-church worship has that sort of impact on youth group graduates when they enter college?

    Q: What are the ramifications for our students while they're still in high school?

Finding 4: Students don't feel that *youth ministries* prepare them for the transition.

Only *15* percent of youth group graduates feel their youth ministry prepared them well for the transition to college. Areas in which students felt particularly unprepared include managing their time, developing Christian friendships on campus, and finding a church. Ask—

Q: **What can we do to prepare students better in these areas?**

Explain: **One way we can help our students is by pointing them to churches or campus ministries at the colleges they'll be attending. Also, online ministries such as www.liveabove.com can help freshmen get connected to ministries, as well as to other believers at their schools.**

How

Continue: **The good news is that we still have time with our seniors. Plus it's not too late to think about how we can connect with those who graduated from our youth ministry this past spring.**

Invite your leaders to form two brainstorming teams and use the space in their *Participant's Guide* to record their ideas. The first team can brainstorm ideas to prepare high school seniors for what they'll face in college. Those ideas can include training sessions for seniors (and their parents) on the transition, panels with real-live college students, or articles you'd like to distribute to students before they leave (the Essential Thoughts article in this chapter, for example).

The second team can brainstorm ways to connect with students who have recently graduated. Possibilities include high-tech social networking sites, medium-tech email updates, and low-tech homemade chocolate chip cookies sent with notes from current youth group kids. After all, who doesn't like to know that their youth group is still thinking of them?

Bring both brainstorming teams back together and ask them to share their ideas. Prioritize among the ideas so you leverage your energy and time toward the ideas that will have the greatest impact.

Invite your leaders to turn to the Essential Impact Action Plan in their *Participant's Guide* and use its rows as a way to pinpoint specific goals, action steps, and prayer requests.

Close in prayer by distributing copies of the lists containing the names of your seniors. Give your leaders time to pray aloud for students by name. Encourage your leaders to keep this list of seniors as a reminder to pray for them on a regular basis. If you'd like you can invite your leaders to

Essential Impact Action Plan

Our team's ideas for how to move forward into essential impact with our seniors and youth group graduates include:

OVERALL GOALS	ACTION STEPS TOWARD THESE GOALS	SPECIFIC PRAYER REQUESTS	SIGNS OF GOD'S ACTIVITY

volunteer to contact a few seniors during the coming week to ask for prayer requests and let them know that your team is praying for them in this final and important year of high school.

ENDNOTES: CHAPTER NINE

Essential Impact: Faith Beyond High School

1. This section is adapted from an article entitled "When the Pomp and Circumstance Fades: A Profile of Youth Group Kids Post-Youth-Group," by Kara Powell and Krista Kubiak, *YouthWorker Journal* (Sept./Oct. 2005).

2. For more on the College Transition Project and its methodology, please visit www.fulleryouthinstitute.org.

For justice work to make a real impact on students, leaders need to spend more time with their students before, during, and after their service. The lessons included in *Deep Justice Journeys* will help you prepare students for what to expect on their mission trip and service work and will allow them to reflect upon their experiences—ensuring justice work that changes students to change the world around them. Also included are ideas to help get parents and the church engaged in the youth ministry's justice work.

Deep Justice Journeys—Leader's Guide
50 Activities to Move from Mission Trips to Missional Living
Kara Powell and Brad M. Griffin
Retail $14.99 | 978-0-310-28603-5

Deep Justice Journeys—Student Journal
Moving from Mission Trips to Missional Living
Kara Powell and Brad M. Griffin
Retail $9.99 | 978-0-310-28773-5

Visit www.youthspecialties.com or your local bookstore.

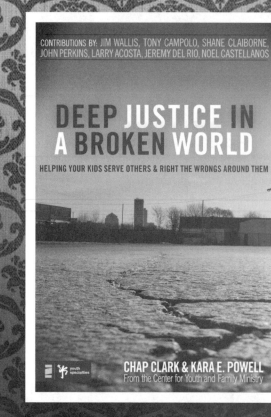

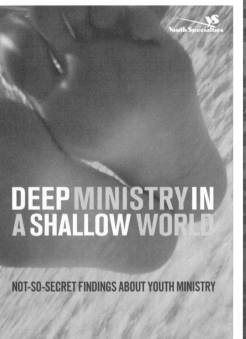

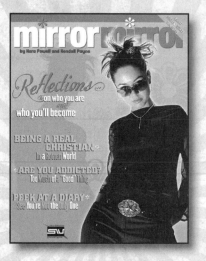

Packed with helpful tips, stories, and biblical advice, *Mirror, Mirror* looks and reads like a magazine and provides teen girls with a God's-eye view on things like make-up, dieting, sex, friends, guys, and more. Self-care and soul-care blend, giving adolescent girls the tools they need to view themselves as children of God.

Mirror, Mirror
Reflections on Who You Are and Who You'll Become

Kara Powell and Kendall Payne
Retail $12.99 | 978-0-310-24886-6